Finding the Bull

Inside the Bear

Active Management Strategies
for *Expansions*, *Contractions*,
and *Everything* in Between

Robert N. Stein

Senior Portfolio Manager and Economist, *Astor Asset Management*
Global Head of Asset Management, *Knight Capital Group, Inc.*

MARKETPLACE BOOKS
COLUMBIA, MARYLAND

DEDICATION

In Memory of My Father, Jerry Stein

April 5, 1929 -- December 5, 2011

--------◆--------

ACKNOWLEDGEMENTS

When sitting down to write a book, it truly becomes a labor of love from so many sources, expected and unexpected. A simple thank you is never enough, but hopefully the meaningful words of gratitude mentioned here will somehow express the appreciation I have for their support.

My colleagues at Astor who work above and beyond the call of duty to give our clients the best service and products are truly dedicated to our cause. On the Astor Team, I wish to thank Jeff Feldman, Bryan Novak, Scott Thomas, Althea Trevor, Brian Durbin, and our intern Patrick Commins. Special thanks go out to Stephanie Yuskis who is my personal GPS.

Of course support outside of business is also very important in completing this project. My family has always been supportive of me in almost all of my endeavors; my wife, Eileen, and my son Spencer are my biggest fans.

I hope all enjoy this book and take away from it a new understanding of the importance of active management and investing, to "find the bull inside the bear."

Thank you,
Rob Stein

TABLE OF CONTENTS

Introduction

THE CASE FOR ACTIVE MANAGEMENT

Over my years as an economist, I have combined in-depth study of the economy and a passion for the markets into a single discipline: investing based on the economic cycle. This enables me, as an investor and portfolio manager, to put the power of the "big picture" behind each investment decision.

From the start of my career as an intern at the Federal Reserve, when Paul Volcker was chairman, to my move to Wall Street, where I was a senior trader for several prestigious banks, I was witness to the value of economic data. Data not only influence the markets, but also determine the overall tone and direction of the economy. I quickly saw that, when making investment decisions, forecasting the economy was not as important as identifying the current stage of the economic cycle. Today, as senior managing director and portfolio manager of Astor Asset Management, LLC, my emphasis remains on the current economic cycle. We use economic analysis to make informed investment decisions through all phases of the economic cycle, from expansion to contraction and back again. This strategy is called active management.

Active management is a general term and may encompass a variety of strategies. The one we will discuss in this book is active management using economic analysis. As we will illustrate throughout this discussion, identification of the current economic environment—as it goes through the four distinct cycles of expansion, peak, contraction, and trough—is paramount to our active strategy. By reviewing and analyzing specific economic data, we can identify the existing cycle for the overall economy or within a particular sector. Once we have confirmed with a high degree of certainty where the economy is, the portfolio selection process becomes much easier.

As history has shown, how the stock market, and therefore investment portfolios, react to economic data and events depends largely on the current economic cycle. When the economy is expanding, it is much easier (and more likely) for the market to shake off bad news. When the economy is contracting, however, that same negative news intensifies the downward momentum. The current economic climate is everything. For example, the so-called stock market "crash" of October 1987 is easily recalled by investors. But how many people remember that stock market averages were actually up for that year? The reason was that the economy, as I define it, was actually expanding. Thus, it was fairly easy for the market to recover from the crash (which was more like a hiccup) and resume its upward momentum.

There are other, similar examples throughout the 1990s: currency defaults, the Russian debt crisis, and the failure of hedge-fund giant Long Term Capital Management. All of these events had only a short-term impact on the market, which eventually recovered due to the fact that the economy was expanding during these times. Had the events occurred against a negative economic backdrop, the result would have been far different. Consider the bursting of the internet bubble in 2000, followed by the horrific events of September 11, 2001, which occurred during an economic contraction. Because of the deteriorating economy at the time, the market reacted more negatively and took longer to recover than if these events had happened under more positive conditions.

A more recent example is the European debt problem, which resurfaced following the "flash crash" of May 2010 in which the Dow Jones Industrial Average dropped more than 1,000 points in a day. The market recovered from both of these negative events and, in the process, put in new post-recession highs within about 90 days. The reason? The economy was growing again. If these events had occurred during an economic contraction, recovery would have taken far longer, and a new post-recession high would not have been established.

The lesson here is to use economic data to construct portfolios that have the best chance of producing a favorable return, and also to use the data to know when to scale back your holdings. In other words, the data will tell you when to "hold 'em" through a relatively short period of market turbulence and when to "fold 'em" because what was bad has just gotten worse.

As we review recent economic history, there were significant events that changed the behavior of the markets forever. The financial crisis of 2008 to 2009 did just that, resulting in permanent changes to financing, bank-to-bank lending, and securitization of loans. The tools of the Fed to navigate around sharp turns have been expanded, as has its balance sheet.

In the wake of the financial crisis, it also appears that the role of government will become more prevalent. This is not a political statement as much as an observation of fact. Each party may go about it differently, but the result will be the same. It appears the tails of risks (and returns) are being chopped off (which is unfortunate, I might add). Returns will eventually look more like utilities. It is clear, at least for now, that risk and loss are intolerable, no matter what the potential reward. In fact, this might be one of the reasons U.S. treasuries are still attracting investor flow.

Regardless of these changes, the longer-term direction of the markets is a function of economic activity. Further, despite counterproductive policies over the decades, capitalism wins. As Adam Smith pointed out, as long as the basic fundamentals of democratic capitalism exist—the division of labor, freedom to trade, and the ability to work for profit—the economy will endure. There will be ups and downs, but this is the best system to allocate resources for overall growth and benefit.

Responding to a New Investment Climate with Active Management

Today, we are in a new investment climate. A distinctive feature of the new climate is the fact that investment cycles are not as pronounced or as long in duration as prior cycles. As a consequence, shorter cycles will have a significant impact on the economic order. Add to that the explosion of information availability and heightened investor awareness of economic developments and news events. With shorter and often less pronounced cycles, investment professionals and their clients must be more vigilant than ever. They need to be astute about the underlying condition of the economy and the likely impact on the stock market. Consequently, they must be agile in both their decision-making and their actions. In other words, in this new investment paradigm, investors need to embrace a new way of approaching and reacting to the market by applying active management.

Active management means taking a proactive approach to investing by utilizing fundamental and technical analysis to create value in a portfolio. This approach allows financial professionals and their clients to make profits in any type of market climate, regardless of market direction, volatility, or bull or bear condition. Using active management, professionals and their clients make investment decisions to either buy (go long) or sell (go short) the market, depending upon a set of predetermined criteria. This is markedly different from buying and holding or constructing a portfolio of supposedly diversified holdings. Furthermore, active management reduces risk by limiting losses during bear markets and providing a better base from which to build profits during bull markets.

The most important issue is for investors to dedicate a portion of their assets to active management. Active management is a necessary strategy to pursue an independent and empowered financial future. Through active management, investors and their advisors are no longer held captive by traditional buy-and-hold strategies, and have an important defense against the vagaries of the stock market.

At Astor Asset Management, our economics-based approach to active management means, in simplest terms, that we buy equities when the economic conditions are most favorable (economic expansion) and sell equities or even taking a short position in the market when the economic conditions dictate (economic contraction). Given today's shorter economic cycles, there are also gradations to our long and short positions. Thus, we must be prepared, depending upon our analysis of the economy and the market, to be 75 to 100 percent long equities at times, and only 25 to 50 percent long at others, depending upon the strength of the cycle. Or, I may take a 25 percent short position in one market, such as the Nasdaq, while retaining a long position in another, such as the S&P 500. It's all determined by vigilantly analyzing economic indicators that signal the current stage of the economy, rather than reacting to the fluctuations of the market and the advice of TV pundits.

One finger must be kept on the pulse of the economy and another on the trigger of investment decisions. Make no mistake: I am not talking about capturing short-term moves that last only a few days. Rather, I am proposing to be nimble enough in one's economic and market analysis and investment decisions to take on long and short positions as conditions dictate.

Being vigilant and flexible—ready to switch from a partially long to a partially short position and back again—will be the only way to reap a positive portfolio return in the years ahead. Those who fail to recognize this fact run the risk of having the gains they reap during the bull markets erased by the ensuing bear-market corrections, and with shorter time frames to recoup their losses. If that happens, where will they be in the end?

Active management is the new investment paradigm for today's economic climate and for the broad base of investors participating in the market. The stock market, once seen as an exclusive club for the wealthy, has more participation than ever before, largely through the proliferation of 401(k) plans and other retirement accounts. Mutual funds, individual stocks, exchange-traded funds (ETFs), and other securities make up the portfolios of more Americans than ever before. With their financial security on the line, these investors have become hyperaware of market conditions, especially given the painful lessons of the financial crisis. Investors who failed to take action in response to changing market and economic conditions paid the price—literally.

My purpose in writing this book is to explain the benefits of active management and how this approach is a vitally important tool for today's investment professionals and their clientele. In upcoming chapters we will address active management and economics-based investment; the principles of economics-based investment; risk and reward and true diversification using ETFs to gain exposure to the broad market and specific sectors; and comparisons of active investment versus buy-and-hold. In addition, we are including our latest outlook, an in-depth look at what's happening in the economy, the markets, and all the factors that influence them. In the Appendix, you will find a calendar template to help you keep track of significant economic events and a glossary of economic terms.

My hope is that, by reading this book, you will come away with a working knowledge of how to put together the pieces of the economic puzzle, and how to turn economic analysis and opinion into informed decisions in the market. Along the way, you'll also gain a clearer understanding of matching risk tolerance and investment objectives through the sheer versatility of active management.

As investors have learned from the recent past, investing is more than merely allocating assets and then walking away to let time perform some sort of magic. Successful investing requires continual study and decisiveness. You don't have to be tuned to the market's every move all day long, but you should monitor a handful of key economic indicators so that you can be aware of shifts and undercurrents in time to react and preserve more of your hard-earned wealth. It is a discipline that cannot be underestimated and, as we all know, its reward is well worth the effort.

Chapter 1

ACTIVE MANAGEMENT AND ECONOMIC REALITY

The challenge we see is convincing investors to pay attention to what is happening now, instead of getting caught up in all the predictions for the future—predictions upon predictions and probabilities upon probabilities.

If there was one, single important lesson to be learned from the latest bear market, it is the value of real diversification. By real diversification we do not mean merely spreading equity exposure around to different types of stocks and adding some fixed-income holdings. The only strategy that has proven viable during bear markets—and the one that holds promise during uptrends as well—is true asset diversification through active management.

At Astor, active management means using economic analysis to determine the most opportune times to buy and sell equities. Namely, we buy during economic expansions and sell, or even short-sell, during economic contractions. We accomplish this by utilizing investment instruments that represent a broad sector of the market, such as the S&P 500 or Nasdaq 100. An effective way to accomplish this objective is with exchange-traded funds (ETFs), which can be used by money managers and individual investors alike to gain exposure to indices and sectors (ETFs will be discussed in greater detail later in the book).

We believe that investing in the broader indices is a far more effective way to profit from opportunities in bull and bear markets than trying to pick individual stocks. Granted, traditional wisdom says that even in a bear market there will be some "good" stocks to buy. In a bull market the majority of stocks go up, although some to a greater degree than others. Picking the right stock for market conditions, however, is far too risky without a commensurate reward. By contrast, applying active management to broader market indices increases an investor's chances of participating in the overall market trends, both up and down.

Certainly equities aren't the only instruments for an active management strategy. There are also approaches for fixed income such as the Active Income Fund that Astor offers clients who are seeking low-risk means to invest in the fixed-income markets.

Given the dominance of equities in most investor portfolios these days, it is extremely important to recognize how active management can produce potentially significant returns that are at least commensurate with the long-term, historical return associated with stocks of 12 percent to 15 percent over time. Active management carries less risk than buying and holding stocks since it eliminates exposure to equities during market corrections. In addition, more aggressive investors can establish short positions in equities to capitalize on market corrections.

Active management is in line with the basic investment concept of "buy low, sell high." After all, this is the fundamental way of making a profit. The vital difference, however, is that active management does not use arbitrary price targets or the fact that the market is up or down at a particular moment to trigger investment actions. Rather, it relies on pre-set criteria—in the case of Astor, the stages of the economic cycle—to make informed, intelligent investment decisions.

As recent bear market corrections have shown us, corrections in the overall stock market can come at the worst time, taking away 50 percent or more of an equity portfolio and wiping away years of gains. Unfortunately, these corrections occur when investors have their largest exposure to stocks, making the corrections feel even greater than their percentages. If you lose 50 percent of your portfolio, you need a gain of 100 percent just to get you back to flat. Based on average returns, this can take you eight to ten years! Therefore, avoiding drawdowns caused by contractions can add years to your investment life.

Active Management—Knowing When to Buy and Sell

To actively manage an account or portfolio, you need criteria for when to buy and when to sell. At Astor, we invest based on the current economic conditions—not what we believe the economy will likely do a few months from now. Over the years, we have found that economic reality is far more powerful than a hypothetical forecast. I learned this lesson when I started my career as an analyst at the Federal Reserve. Part of my job was to compile economic data, dealing with tangibles such as the rate of growth of GDP, weekly jobless claims, and the size of the U.S. workforce.

When I moved to Wall Street, I took on a much more difficult job: forecasting. The problem with forecasting was that I was wrong a lot. It's like the old joke that says economists were created to make weather forecasters look good. Very quickly I returned to my analytical roots. Rather than trying to predict what was going to happen, I preferred to review and analyze economic data to determine what was happening at the time. Specifically, I wanted to create criteria to determine the current stage of the business cycle. Once the business cycle was identified, an active management investment strategy could be implemented to capitalize on a particular stage. Focusing on economic cycle identification, rather than making investment decisions based on market timing or predictions that typically have a low percentage of accuracy, is a cornerstone of the Astor investment philosophy.

The Business Cycle

Determining the current phase of the business cycle is not without its challenges. For one thing, economic signals can be mixed, and the economy can grow or contract at different rates at different times. The objective, therefore, is to look at specific economic data, which I will review later in this chapter, and make a determination of where the economy is at the moment.

At any given time, the economy is at one of our sequential phases of the business cycle: expansion, peak, contraction, or trough. Repeated over and over through the decades, the business cycle looks like the sine wave in Figure 1.1, rising higher, peaking out, declining, hitting

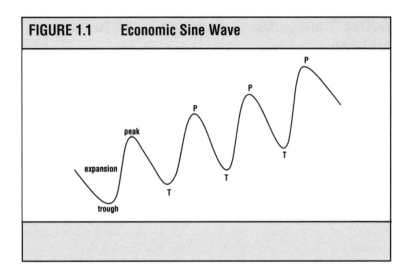

FIGURE 1.1   Economic Sine Wave

bottom, and rising again. The overall direction of the wave is upward, with higher peaks and higher bottoms, as the U.S. economy moves steadily forward.

Let's take a look at each of these four phases and the characteristics of each.

- Expansion usually lasts the longest of all the economic stages and produces the greatest amount of wealth. This phase is marked by low unemployment and higher corporate profits, which usually lead to stock market rallies. In simplest terms, when more people are working, producing more things, and investing more money, the economy is expanding.

- Peak is the euphoria stage during which stock prices appreciate sharply and consumer spending surges. This is also when companies tend to overbuild, overbuy, and over-hire. Excesses build up that are not healthy for the economy in the long run.

- Contraction may be an unpleasant stage, but it is a very necessary one. As the economy slows down or slips into recession, businesses begin to shed the excesses that resulted from expansion and peak stages. Consumer spending and investment decrease. Companies lay off workers and stock prices decline.

Contraction is the mirror opposite of expansion. In simplest terms, it means fewer people working, less is being made, and declining investments.

- Trough is when the contraction hits bottom. Large numbers of workers are laid off, and consumer spending declines. Although the economy is still contracting during the trough, companies that are leaner and more efficient start to make money again. Lower labor costs and higher worker productivity (the result of earlier layoffs) help boost corporate profits. This allows the economy to get healthy again and returns the cycle back to expansion.

Defining the Business Cycle in Real Time

The business cycle is easiest to identify in the rearview mirror. With the passage of time, economists study not only the current economic data, but also the latest numbers in the context of previous data. That's why the National Bureau of Economic Research (NBER) makes its pronouncements on the beginning and the end of a recession months after the fact.

From an active management standpoint, the challenge is determining how the economy is performing right now. Do the data indicate an expanding economy or a contracting one? Are the data mixed, indicating the next phase is not fully underway? Although there is a plethora of data by which to analyze the economy—from durable goods to vehicle sales to housing market statistics and reports from regional Federal Reserve banks—at Astor we have broken it down to the ABCs of economic analysis:

- GDP (Gross Domestic Product)
- Employment
- Investment money flows and stock price momentum

Using this data we determine if more people are working (as measured by employment statistics) and making more products (as measured by GDP), and investing more money (as measured by money flows and stock price momentum). If so, then the economy is expanding. Conversely, if fewer people are working, making fewer products and investing less, then the economy is contracting.

Let's take a closer look at each of these components of our economic analysis.

GDP

Gross Domestic Product is one of the most comprehensive measures of economic health, reflecting the physical output of businesses. To get technical just for a moment, GDP reflects the sum of consumption, investment, government spending, and exports, minus imports. Of these components, the largest is consumption, accounting for about two-thirds of the total. Little wonder then, that consumer spending is so closely watched. Even though GDP is a lagging indicator that is subject to revision, it is a vitally important gauge of the U.S. economy that is watched by everyone from the Federal Reserve Board of Governors to traders on the floor of the stock exchange. Granted, GDP does have some limitations. For example, it tends to understate the service and technology sectors, and it subtracts from U.S. output the goods and components imported into the U.S. by American multinationals from their overseas operations. Nonetheless, since those limitations are consistent quarter-to-quarter, GDP acts like an index, reflecting the relative strength or weakness of the economy.

You don't have to be an economist to decipher GDP or to understand what's happening in the economy. When a GDP report is released, the first questions to be considered are:

- How is the economy performing compared to the previous quarter?

- How does the economy compare to a year ago?

- Is the GDP rate of growth increasing, which would indicate relative improvement in the economy?

- Or, is the rate of growth declining, which shows that economic growth has slowed?

Occasionally, GDP "goes negative," showing a quarterly growth rate such as -1.0 percent. Obviously, that doesn't mean industrial plants have kicked into reverse and are now "unmaking" goods. Rather, the rate of production has declined in the most recent period from the previous quarter. A negative GDP reading is a sure sign of a contract-

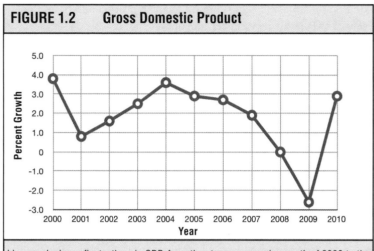

FIGURE 1.2 Gross Domestic Product

Line graph shows fluctuations in GDP, from the strong economic growth of 2000 to the contraction during the 2008 to 2009 recession when GDP "went negative."

ing economy, as reflected by the 2009 reading in Figure 1.2. By classic definition, a recession occurs when there are two sequential negative GDP quarterly numbers. Increasing unemployment and declining stock prices, which can be just as painful as a classic recession, also characterize economic contractions.

Another insight that can be gleaned from the GDP report is the level of inventories. Inventories are not part of the GDP equation since goods in the warehouse today were previously counted as output. However, the report does make note of inventory levels, which can influence the interpretation of the GDP number. For example, a strong GDP output number looks less rosy if growth in output resulted in higher inventories instead of increased consumer or end user sales. Furthermore, when inventories decline because consumption has increased, it is a sign that economic activity may be picking up soon.

Employment

Employment has broad impact beyond the immediate economic implications. Who has a job, who does not, and who is still looking are all important and emotional considerations for the economy. People who have lost their jobs or who are afraid of losing them are reluctant consumers and far less likely to commit to any big-ticket purchases. Jobless fears can also sour investor sentiment.

Employment is such an integral part of the economy that it is specifically mentioned by the Federal Reserve in its goals of monetary policy. In addition, employment is tied directly to the business cycle. In a contracting economy, growth in demand slows and inventories build. Companies cut back production and lay off workers. This helps companies to reduce their labor costs, become more efficient, and improve profitability. During a recession, worker productivity (output per employee) typically improves. As the economy recovers and demand picks up, companies can benefit from lower labor costs for a time. Eventually, however, demand will reach the point at which production must be expanded and additional workers hired. Initially, productivity will decline. However, expansion in payrolls signals that economic recovery is underway.

What's most significant about productivity after an economic contraction is the degree to which the benefits linger. For example, let's say a company has 100 workers making 100 widgets a day. When the economy contracts and demand slackens off, the company is forced to lay off workers. At first, there are 70 workers making 70 widgets a day, and then 50 workers making 60 widgets a day. This initial productivity increase is to be expected, but it's nothing to get excited about because output is still down. When demand picks up, the company may be able to produce 70 widgets with those 50 workers before it must start hiring again. If the company has truly improved productivity, it will be able to increase production at a faster rate than it must hire workers. For example, if production eventually goes up to 150 widgets produced by 100 workers, perhaps through more efficient manufacturing processes or better use of technology, that's a significant productivity improvement. Although contractions are painful, they can often result in better and healthier economic growth in the long run.

To decipher what's happening to the economy in terms of employment, attention is focused on the monthly Employment Situation Report (known unofficially as the unemployment report). When this report is released, the statistic that gets the most attention is the unemployment rate. The absolute statistic is not as important as the relative change from one month to the next and over a longer period of time. Figure 1.3

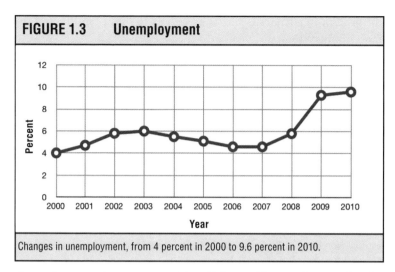

FIGURE 1.3 Unemployment

Changes in unemployment, from 4 percent in 2000 to 9.6 percent in 2010.

shows the unemployment rate rising fairly steadily over the past decade. But another key statistic is the size of payroll employment, which reflects the rise or fall in the number of people working. Additionally, the report shows the number of newly unemployed persons —those who have been out of a job for less than five weeks.

The Employment Report is carefully tracked not only for what it reveals about the current labor market, but also for indications of how well or poorly the economy is performing. Increased joblessness, an increase in the number of newly unemployed persons, and a shrinking payroll number are all indications of poor or weakening economic conditions. Similarly, an uptick in job creation, a decrease in the number of newly unemployed people, and growth in the payroll number are signs of economic improvement. Keep in mind that the economy needs to add about one million jobs a year to keep growing, taking into account both new entries and people leaving the workforce.

Investment Money Flows and Stock Price Momentum

Investment money flows and stock price momentum reveal the underlying belief of how well the economy is performing. Typically, investor sentiment improves in step with economic growth and a better employment picture. The stock market, in fact, is one of the most important indicators of economic activity, reflecting the outlook for growth in corporate output as well as the profitability and the mood of investors.

When analyzing the stock market, we are not concerned at all about price-to-earnings (P/E) ratios. Although some analysts use P/E to suggest whether a stock is underpriced, fairly valued or overpriced, we don't put much credence in this ratio at all. Whether a stock is priced at $50 or $100 means little. Far more important is the relative change in stock prices, particularly when looking at the broader market. That's why we focus on the direction of money flows and stock price momentum.

It is far more important to know if additional investor money is going into equities and increasing the value of the stock market as reflected in the major indices such as the Dow, S&P 500, or the Nasdaq Composite. Or are investors pulling out of equities, causing stock prices to decline? In some instances, the stock market's behavior may be more telling than the economic data, particularly when the economy is perceived to be at or near a turning point in the trend—in other words at the peak or the trough.

When studying economic data or stock market performance, it is important to look beyond just a single report or a one-month time frame. Trends develop over time, and it often takes several months for a new trend to be identified and confirmed. With a longer-term perspective, the goal is to look for a consensus among the indicators, not only to confirm the trend, but also to gauge its strength. For example, when economic indicators show strong growth and the stock market is exhibiting positive upward momentum, the conditions favor a sustained economic expansion. Conversely, when economic indicators worsen and the stock market turns downward, the stage is set for a sustained contraction.

Participating in the Broad Market

Once the current business cycle is identified, an investment strategy can be put in place. Although these strategies have many variations, depending upon factors from the age of the investor to his or her risk tolerance, there are two basic investment premises that should be followed.

1. An expanding economy is favorable to equity markets and therefore owning stocks.

2. A contracting economy is unfavorable for equities, and therefore stocks should be sold and/or short positions taken, and/or allocations to bonds and cash should be increased.

The best way to establish a long or short position in the equity market to capitalize on the current economic condition using an active management strategy is with the broad indices. The indices allow investors to participate in the stock market's moves, both bullish and bearish. These indices, such as the S&P 500 and the Nasdaq 100, are better surrogates for the U.S. economy than any one particular stock.

That is not to say that stocks do not have a place in an investor's portfolio. Many investors buy stocks that they like or that they purchase because of potential growth in a particular sector of the economy. When it comes to active management, however, I believe the best way to capture the movements of the overall economy is with broad-based indices such as the S&P 500 or Nasdaq 100. Keep in mind that active management involves a portion of an investor's portfolio, and may account for 40 to 60 percent of an investor's equity holdings. Depending upon the portfolio mix, this may be as little as 20 or as much as 40 percent of the overall portfolio.

It is also important to realize that the primary determinant of a stock's movement is the underlying direction and momentum of the broader equity market. In fact, industry data show the market itself may account for nearly 80 percent of a stock's movement. Therefore, it is more efficient and effective to participate in the broad market through a stock index rather than an individual stock. An index, by definition, will reflect a large sector of the economy. This cannot be accomplished with any confidence by picking individual stocks. Even in a roaring bull market, there is always the chance that the one stock an investor picks is a laggard.

The Active Management Advantage

For the investment professional, active management strategies are valuable tools for delivering performance to clients, with fewer headaches during the downturns. Further, when the downside risk during corrections is limited (or potentially eliminated altogether), clients have a stronger base on which to build compared with buy-and-hold.

STANDARD & POOR'S 500 (S&P 500)[1]: A basket of 500 widely held stocks, weighted by market value and performance. The index is designed to be representative of the stock market as a whole. Company stocks are selected for the index based on their market size, liquidity, and sector (such as financial, technology, etc.). The S&P 500 is widely used to judge overall U.S. market performance and as a benchmark for performance used by portfolio managers and investment professionals.

NASDAQ 100[2]: A weighted index of the top 100 non-financial stocks traded on the Nasdaq Stock Market. The Nasdaq 100 is a narrower index than the Nasdaq Composite, which reflects the value of all the stocks traded on the Nasdaq. Dominated by the leading, large-cap technology stocks, the Nasdaq 100 is often used as a benchmark for technology-stock performance.

---

1   S&P 500 is a registered trademark of Standard and Poor's.

2   Nasdaq 100 is a registered trademark of The Nasdaq Stock Market, Inc.

The key to active management is that it offers strategies whereby investors can potentially avoid most of the drawdowns by getting out of equities during adverse economic times, or even taking a short position to capitalize on a declining market. Although investors will not catch every up-move in the market as they switch from a short to a long position when economic analysis dictates, they will not need to. Over time, their losses will be smaller, and investors will be allowed to reap profits from short positions during market corrections, while holding profitable long positions during market appreciation.

As part of economics-based active management, it is important to let the analysis do the work it is supposed to do. In other words, you cannot become so wedded to ideas or perceptions of what you think is happening, or what you think should be happening, that you fail to do the analysis or take it seriously. That does not mean you make an investment decision based on every piece of new economic data. Rather, you must always survey the economic landscape to determine what is happening. When that picture is mixed or the data are unclear, do not be afraid to sit on the sidelines until you can determine the economic trend with more confidence. There is nothing wrong with being out of the market and in cash until you feel more certain of what the economic data and stock market performance are telling you.

When in doubt, get the heck out. That's a good mantra for the active investor and for professionals who advise them. No money was ever lost by being in cash. If it turned out you sold too soon, then all you did was forsake some potential profit. If you wait on the sidelines too long before getting in, you can still make significant profits as the trend continues. Consider what happened after the 1990 to 1991 recession. If you had waited until late 1994 or early 1995 before taking a position in equities—missing three years of the expansion—you still would have tripled your money in the S&P 500 and made ten times your money in the Nasdaq. That is, if you did one thing: sell when the expansion ended.

Investing Based on Economics

Taking an economics-based active management approach provides firm rationale and a more precise strategy for making investment decisions. The strategy relies upon underlying economic trends, not merely the fact that a particular stock or sector looks good at the moment. If the economy is expanding, it is a good time to be invested in equities, including higher-risk issues that tend to perform best during these times. When the economy is contracting, it is better to be out of equities and in defensive issues or, for a more aggressive approach, to have a short position in equities.

During these overall trends, there will be countermoves. In every sustained rally, there are periods of time when the market sells off, either as a short-term reaction to news or as profits are taken. Nonetheless, the market will follow the longer-term direction until a new trend is established. For example, from 1995 through 2000, the U.S. saw a period of strong economic growth, solid employment, and higher stock prices. Taking a long position in equities during that time would have yielded excellent results. During that time there were some pullbacks and declines due to a variety of factors and events. Geopolitical and economic upheaval, however, proved to be short-term bumps, and the market found footing each time and continued to move higher.

Economic Expansion
GDP — Sequential quarterly growth starting at a rate of 3.75 percent or better.
Employment — Average monthly job growth of 125,000, or sustained over a quarter.
Stock Market — Continual quarterly appreciation at a 9 to 10 percent annualized growth rate.
Economic Contraction
GDP — Average quarterly growth rate below 3 percent, or sequential lower rates.
Employment — Job losses over three or more months.
Stock Market — Annualized growth rate below risk-free rate of interest, for several quarters.

The challenge is always to discern the trend, despite outside forces, particularly at moments when the data are unclear or an economic change has been detected. To do that, investment professionals should make a habit of studying economic data—month-to-month and quarter-to-quarter—in order to ascertain if the prevailing economic trend is still intact, or if the trend is beginning to change. Here are some examples from recent history to illustrate.

In early 2000, a roaring economy and long bull run in the stock market made many people wonder if we would ever see a bear market again. By the first quarter of 2000, however, there were signs of what was to come. GDP, which had been up a whopping 7.3 percent in the fourth quarter of 1999, dropped to a 5.5 percent gain in the first quarter of 2000. Similarly, the stock market (as measured by the monthly close for the Dow Jones Industrial Average) also began dropping, from a December 1999 close of 11,497.12 to the March 2000 close of 10,921.90. The writing was on the wall, but how many people paid attention? By the third quarter of 2000, with GDP showing 2.2 percent and the stock market continuing to drop, it was becoming apparent that the long expansion of the 1990s was coming to a close.

A few years later, many investors would be surprised again when economic expansion came to an end. Had they been looking for signs, however, they would have headed for cover. In the fourth quarter of 2007, despite warnings of a housing market bubble, few people expected the bloodbath that would occur amid the credit crunch that became a full-blown financial crisis. Yet, once again, the economic statistics would have been an early warning signal.

By the fourth quarter of 2007, GDP was slowing, up 0.6 percent. The stock market closed the year at 13,264.82, down 4.5 percent from the third quarter, but still 7.4 percent higher than the first quarter close. By mid-2008, however, the statistics told a different story, as Table 1.1 illustrates. In the first quarter of 2008, GDP came in at 0.9 percent, followed by a small reprieve as the economy gained of 2.8 percent in the second quarter of 2008. The economy then fell sharply with readings of 0.5 percent in the third quarter of 2008 and -6.3 percent in the fourth quarter. Two quarters of contraction as measured by GDP is the classic definition of a recession.

The Employment Situation report, meanwhile, showed steep job losses, which accelerated throughout 2008, as shown in Table 1.2. In the fourth quarter of 2008 alone, job losses were 1,297,000.

No surprise then, that the stock market also declined sharply, falling to a monthly close at the end of the fourth quarter of 8,776.39 as seen in Table 1.3, a level that had not been seen since early 2003.

The economic contraction continued through mid-2009, as evidenced by GDP numbers. The stock market reflected the deep concerns for the economy, although as conditions seemed to improve from the depths of carnage in the first quarter of 2009, the Dow did recover somewhat from its lows. Job losses continued, although not at the magnitude of early 2009.

By the third quarter of 2009, the economy was growing again. Job losses continued throughout 2009, although growth in employment did resume in 2010 (with some losses in the third quarter of 2010). As one would expect, the stock market also recovered from its lows, ending 2009 above 10,000, and staying above that level for the majority of 2010.

TABLE 1-1 GDP by Quarters

	Q1	Q2	Q3	Q4
2007	0.7	3.8	4.9	0.6
2008	0.9	2.8	-0.5	-6.3
2009	-6.4	-0.7	2.2	5.6
2010	3.7	1.7	2.6	3.1

TABLE 1-2 Employment Situation Change in Nonfarm Payroll

	Q1	Q2	Q3	Q4
2007	388,000	377,000	291,000	278,000
2008	-160,000	-131,000	294,000	-1,297,000
2009	-1,912,000	-1,351,000	-726,000	-286,000
2010	106,000	596,000	-280,000	293,000

TABLE 1-3 Stock Market (as measured by the month close for the Dow)

	Q1	Q2	Q3	Q4
2007	12,354.35	13,408.62	13,895.63	13,264.82
2008	12,262.89	11,350.01	10,850.66	8,776.39
2009	7,609.00	8,447.00	9,712.28	10,428.05
2010	10,856.63	9,774.02	10,788.05	11,577.51

Economics in Action

Economic statistics are dynamic. Not only do they change from month to month and quarter to quarter, but they also ebb and flow with the pulse of U.S. business and the market. You don't have to be an economist to decipher economic statistics. Reading, understanding, and tracking a few key statistics over a period of time will yield insights into how the economy is performing, what the prevailing trend is, and if the trend is changing. With this insight, investment professionals can help their clients make better and more informed decisions, with greater confidence, as part of an overall strategic plan.

Chapter 2

OUTLOOK 2012: IT'S ALL ABOUT THE MONEY

At Astor Asset Management, we begin the New Year with a backward look at where we've been in order to put into perspective the events, forces, and other factors that will influence the next twelve months. Following is a recap of how we view the economic landscape for 2011 and what lies ahead for 2012.

Without a doubt, 2011 was one of the most challenging years for portfolio managers, and this manager for sure, given the extreme volatility of the market. The Dow Jones Industrial Average frequently saw daily moves of several hundred points in both directions, depending upon the day and the headlines du jour. When you strip out those gyrations, you can see that not much really happened. The S&P 500 ended the year at 1257.60, just on the negative side of flat from where we started the year.

I am proud of how well the Astor team identified the impact of economic events, even if some of our trade executions were sub-optimal. We began 2011 with the economy expanding, albeit at a rate that was slower than hoped for at the time. The fundamentals early in the year certainly supported further economic growth and continued equity appreciation. As we moved forward into the year, however, the markets appeared to rally more robustly than perhaps could be justified by the fundamentals in the third year of a recovery following the great recession of 2008. One unforeseen event that struck the economy at a vulnerable time was the tragic earthquake and tsunami that hit Japan late in the first quarter of 2011, followed by a catastrophic nuclear accident. With the third largest economy in the world and a major source of capital essentially offline, it is no wonder that the global economy felt the blow. For the U.S., the timing could not have been worse, as the domestic recovery had finished its second year and was getting long in the tooth. The U.S. economy needed fresh support, not new headwinds, for the recovery to continue apace. By mid-year 2011, the economic data were waning, with growth in GDP slowing to 1.3 percent in the second quarter and unemployment persisting around the 9.0 percent mark. At mid-year, we believed that the economy had hit the "stall speed"—meaning it was growing, but at such a slow pace it put further growth into question and raised the possibility of another economic recession.

Our decision was to take risk off the table and reduce equity exposure. With the benefit of 20/20 hindsight we can see that we made the right call regarding the economy. One of our investment choices, however, was high-yield fixed income, based on our belief that corporate balance sheets were in better shape than government balance sheets. Unfortunately, at the time, novice investors were drawn in by advertisements from brokerage firms that touted high-dividend securities and low broker loan rates as safe bets. Then came the Washington political drama, with trumped up fears over the debt ceiling and a downgrade of the U.S. federal government's debt rating from Triple-A to double A-plus. (In our view, the downgrade by S&P was ludicrous since the ability of the U.S. to repay its debts had not changed one iota.)

The general public misunderstood the debt ceiling debate and panicked over media projections of what could happen if the U.S. government could not issue more debt to keep the wheels turning. In an atmosphere of sell first and ask questions later, investors bailed out of everything. Some fixed income assets lost more than their equity counterparts. Our portfolios suffered slightly in this massacre, as well. Adding fuel to an already hot fire was the European debt issue, with a multi-month Greek drama as that country teetered on the brink of default several times while the European Union hammered together a bailout plan.

Removing the political drama and the hype of projections, we can see that the economy did start to stutter step at mid-year. It was clear that GDP was going to come in at the lower end of the projected range, due largely to reduced government spending (which is usually a 20+ percent contributor to GDP) and lower prospects for exports to Europe. While many money managers pointed to strong earnings and large profit margins, which would eventually send markets higher, we believed that these conditions were only supporting the market and keeping it from crashing.

Corporate America has done a great job of repairing balance sheets, raising cash, and becoming more efficient, but that has not been enough to spur demand and create jobs. Therefore, in the second half of the year, we became even more defensive and focused on reducing volatility. Again, our decision proved to be correct, because the fourth quarter of 2011 saw even greater daily swings in the markets. Because of our defensive positioning, volatility in our portfolios was a mere fraction of what was experienced in the market. However, the timing of that decision locked in returns that did not show our proudest moment.

Most important, however, we stuck to our discipline and philosophy to create our investment portfolio. We can't worry about how we got here. We began the fourth quarter of 2011 with the best portfolio for the conditions at the time, with low volatility and reduced risk compared to any competing portfolio to which we are compared for that period. As 2011 came to a close, it's clear that there was a lot of noise for the past 12 months, but little to show otherwise, fundamentally and statistically from a return standpoint. And as we look back on 2011 sans the political drama, we are able to see clearly what we believe lies ahead.

2012 Outlook

The theme for 2012 is "it's all about the money." Never before have we heard so much political rhetoric, both domestically and abroad, centered on the economy and, more specifically, about money. Every problem has a price tag associated it, one way or another. This costs too much…Raise taxes…Lower taxes…Spend less… etc. You'd think that money issues were the only ones in the U.S. or the world. Consider the U.S. war in Iraq, which essentially came to an end with little fanfare on either side, pro or con. What about global warming, food supplies, homeland security, global terrorist threats, the need to improve education domestically and around the world, and many other issues besides?

Our current obsession with money has a lot to do with the great recession of 2008. The financial crisis that touched it off was caused by the misuse of money and exacerbated by easy credit that spurred borrowing. Then came overspending and excessive debt that accumulated over several years. We can't lay the blame on one over-extended consumer group or bad mortgage practices or government spending programs. Rather, as I will discuss shortly, the root of our ills is the consistent misuse of personal balance sheets over an extended period of time.

To listen to the current rhetoric, however, one might think that money is the cure for whatever ails us. If people and corporations simply earn more (buy more, invest more) then we'll be out of the woods and back on easy street. Not so. Yet, our myopic thinking keeps us from seeing anything except money—and more specifically jobs and money. (By the way, what I see being done in the name of money indicates to me we need to rethink our value system, but that's another story.) And while we're at it, when did every politician become an economist and with conviction to boot? Rather than relying on the best economic minds in the country with a nonpartisan study and recommendations, lawmakers have their own opinions, thank you very much, along with what they think are all the answers to cure the current economic malaise. The solution, however, is not more money; it's less debt.

Regardless of what one's opinion might be about the actions of the central banks and the governments during the financial crisis and the ensuing recession (the pros and cons of which we can debate forever), all sides must agree on one thing: the result was to buy time. Some will say the Fed and central bankers around the world merely "kicked the can down the road" and that the day of reckoning will come, sooner or later. Yet buying time is not a bad outcome given where we were and where we are now, three years later. Yes, there were a lot of foreclosures and job losses. Buying time, however, essentially allowed people to regroup and repair. Of the three key sectors—public, private, and corporate— the best use of that time was made by corporations. Corporate America reduced payrolls, cut expenses, and shored up its balance sheets. Now, corporations, in general, are sitting on a good deal of cash. Thus, I have few worries about the financial health of U.S. corporations. Unlike the shaky days of 2008, I don't foresee another wave of large companies getting into trouble and possibly going out of business.

Public debt in the U.S. also is not a major concern for me. Of course, I am cognizant of what has happened in Europe, with the threat of default on sovereign debt leaving governments between the rock of austerity and the hard place of tax increases. Some local debt in the U.S. is also problematic. However, I do not see widespread problems where governmental debt in the U.S. is concerned. The U.S. is not Europe—not even close—on so many levels, including a bigger base of earners. Although some concerns are being voiced out there about U.S. debt as a percentage of GDP, I am not ready to sound the alarm. If we do get into dangerous territory, we will have plenty of time to avert a crisis.

The real problem, as the charts below will illustrate, is the private sector. Consumers ruined their personal balance sheets by essentially consuming ten years' worth of stuff in five years. Consumer household debt levels, which reached a peak of 130 percent in the third quarter of 2007, have eased somewhat to 114 percent of after-tax income as of the first quarter of 2011, but remain elevated. Housing has yet to recover, and 30 percent of U.S. homeowners owe more than their houses are worth, to the tune of about 15 million borrowers and almost one trillion dollars in mortgage debt. With consumer spending accounting for nearly 70 percent of GDP, this alone should make 2012 challenging. Now, as consumers deleverage, the necessary reduction in spending will be another drag on the economy, which is already on thin ice.

What's the Problem? My Financial Picture, That's What!

The last decade has been challenging from an investment standpoint as investors have experienced two separate recessions, first in 2002 and then in 2008, each accompanied by a peak-to-valley drawdown in stocks of more than 50 percent. The last recession was accompanied by an even more destructive economic force for consumers as home prices, according to the Case-Shiller Index, fell more than 30 percent from their peak in 2006. This combination has made the recession of 2008 the worst economic downturn since the Great Depression, followed by a difficult recovery. Yet, even with all these challenges, prudent and consistent consumers had the opportunity to weather the storm and create some value for themselves. While not spared the losses and effects of this past recession, those who had stayed the course may have a far better investment portfolio and total wealth picture than they otherwise would have had, as illustrated in Figure 2.1.

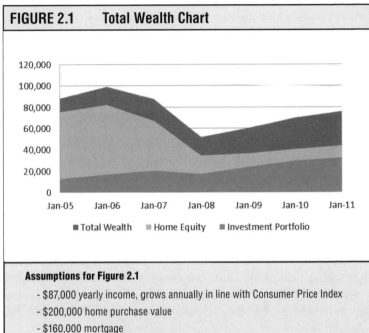

FIGURE 2.1   Total Wealth Chart

Assumptions for Figure 2.1
- $87,000 yearly income, grows annually in line with Consumer Price Index
- $200,000 home purchase value
- $160,000 mortgage
- $10,000 initial investment portfolio
- 2.5% savings/investment rate
- Investment portfolio split 70/30 between S&P 500 and Barclays Aggregate Bond Index

Given the turmoil of the past six years, being prudent paid off for those who stuck to a simple plan of no additional debt beyond a reasonable mortgage (i.e., living within one's means) and consistently contributing to investment accounts for long-term goals. While home values have fallen, which has reduced home equity, maintaining a consistent investment plan has resulted in a portfolio that is significantly higher, thanks to regular contributions and investing at lower market levels. Although this scenario is not ideal, and not having higher total wealth over a seven-year period is not the typical investor plan, it is livable—particularly when you consider the alternative.

Unfortunately, the overwhelming majority of us do not fit the profile of being consistently prudent. Living "in the moment," as opposed to thinking longer term, affects decision making, as we all know. Thus, in addition to declining home prices and a volatile stock market, many consumers are feeling the effects of having increased their debt levels over this period. Consumer debt-to-income ratios, while declining from 2006 levels, still stand above 100 percent, which is considered very high from a historical standpoint, as illustrated in Figure 2.2.

As illustrated, the trouble stemmed from consumers taking out loans against their home equity, which either went back into improvement projects or that were spent elsewhere, all of which negatively impacted total wealth levels. Many people also reduced or stopped contributing to long-term investment portfolios or changed investment amounts and patterns, reduced exposure at unfavorable levels, and didn't make up their portfolio losses when the market rebounded (negative compounding), or all of the above. The bottom line from this comparison is clear: being prudent and consistent would have better served consumers through this period.

What's clear from this study is that the culprit for the loss of wealth during the past decade has not been the stock market or even the hous-

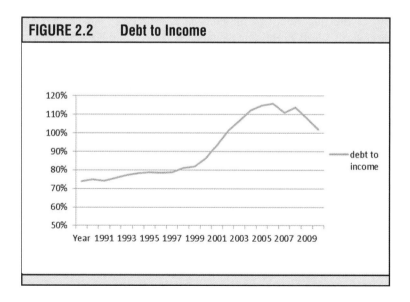

FIGURE 2.2   Debt to Income

ing market. The real problem is debt. Over the past decade, consumers mismanaged their personal balance sheets, investing inappropriately, taking on too much or too little risk, and borrowing from appreciating assets to buy depreciating ones. In effect, they created an appreciating liability on a depreciating asset.

In addition, for consumers in debt, it's not just a matter of tightening belts and cutting back expenses. The bitter pill of deleveraging carries little satisfaction. Buying a shiny new car or taking the entire family on a vacation carries with it a feel-good afterglow. But pay off a mortgage and what do you have to show for your money? You already have the "thing" that you spent the money on (car, boat, house, etc.). All you have now is the pain without a commensurate gain—except for an incrementally healthier balance sheet. After the spree, now it's time to pay the proverbial piper, and it's not going to be cheap—or easy.

The Money "V"

In the aftermath of the financial crisis, much has been made about the role of money in economic forecasting. During the early phases of the economic recovery, increases in the Fed balance sheet were thought to be inflationary, which sent investors rushing out to buy hard assets such as gold. Then it was thought that the U.S. dollar would lose its prominence, and investors fled the greenback. Neither of these trades has been particularly promising. Nonetheless, there are those who forecast the economy and outlook for many assets by looking at the velocity, or "V", of money. The velocity of money (no matter which matrix you use) tells much of the story. It tells why inflation is low and likely to remain low, perhaps even slipping to a deflationary environment temporarily. In addition, it tells why growth is below trend and likely to remain so, and why equity market appreciation will remain subpar as well. Once the velocity of money expands, a sustainable expansion will follow. When and why is a guess; it just doesn't appear to be in 2012.

Currently, the V of money (as illustrated in Figures 2.3, 2.4, and 2.5) is near historical lows—meaning money is not circulating very much through the economy. In the good ol' days, a dollar went through the economy far more frequently than now. You earned a dollar, you bought a skateboard, the guy who made and sold skateboards paid his rent, the

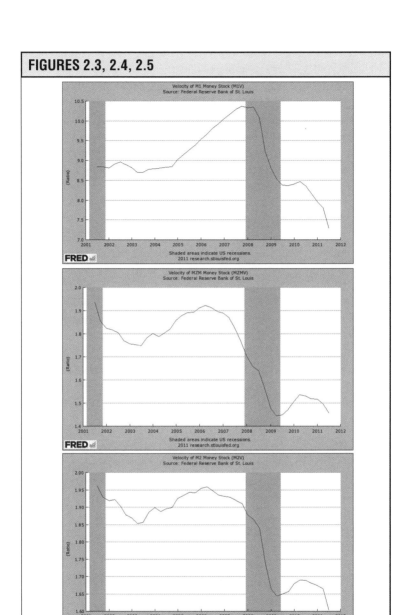

Money supply and money velocity charts show decline in the aftermath of the financial crisis and recession.

landlord bought a new snow blower, the hardware store purchased more inventory, and so forth as money went through a growing economy. More recently, however, money has not been circulating through the system. The reason is simple: more dollars are being used to pay off debt rather than to fuel new purchases. Dollars that are used to deleverage are considered "retired." Typically that would give banks more incentive to initiate additional new loans. Instead, as deleveraging continues, money is not being created at the same rate as it has historically. This, to me, is a sign that economic growth will be subpar.

Stock Market–It's About Valuations

At this point, let's turn our attention to the stock market and what we might see in 2012 from an investment perspective. As the New Year begins, it is clear that companies with strong fundamentals and balance sheets should weather the storm relatively well even as the economy rolls over from modest expansion to contraction. In other words, this is not 2008 all over again. It could get bumpy for equities in early 2012, but the range of the past two years should hold up, at least on a monthly closing basis. I expect that statement to hold true for upside as well as downside projections. There is the risk that we could see a stock market decline, but given the foreseeable circumstances, a 50 percent correction is highly unlikely.

If we do see some economic growth and/or market appreciation, we believe it will be in the latter part of the year after election uncertainty is removed, regardless of which party wins. Further, Fed policies and investor behavior may start to pay some dividends by then—particularly if the money locked in the banking system begins to expand as the money multiplier or velocity reverts back to historical levels. This will happen at some point and the global economy awash with frozen liquidity will usher in a period of significant growth. It will most likely surprise on the upside, so investors need to make sure they are not chewed up by current adverse market behavior.

To that end, what is worth watching is a shift in the typical pattern we've seen thus far. Equities have rallied on every shred of good news, while bonds have gone lower. Conversely, negative news has hit equities and boosted bonds, following the traditional risk on/risk off pattern.

If, at some point, bonds go lower for reasons other than "risk on" and equities follow suit, I would suggest that this is a warning shot that needs to be heeded. It could very well signal that there is perceived risk in U.S. Treasuries, while a slowing economy is hampering stocks. I'm not talking about the Dow being down 50 points and bonds being off a quarter-point. The magnitude I'm referring to is a 300-plus point drop in the Dow in one day and bonds falling by a point. A simultaneous decline in stocks and bonds will be the warning sign that the next leg of the contraction or bear market is upon us, and that the slowdown in the economy is about to get more severe.

We are also about to enter into a climatic shift with regard to valuations. Currently, the S&P 500 tends to trade somewhere between 12 and 20 times earnings. There are opinions out there that by the time the recession or contraction is finally over, the multiple will be in the single digits. This reasoning is not obvious, given the fact that corporations have lots of cash and they are earning plenty of money. Therefore, the idea that stock prices will likely go down when companies are earning money seems contradictory. The answer, however, lies in the fact that the value of stocks is a multiple of cash flow, a concept I always thought was arbitrary to begin with. Why would a company be valued at $1 billion when it makes $100 million? I have never been able to rationalize that relationship, and I've built a business that doesn't need to know those elements of valuation. Instead, I choose to focus on the direction of the economy, which is much more logical and meaningful. When the economy is expanding, stocks tend to appreciate regardless of their multiples. Conversely, when the economy is contracting, stocks tend to decline, even if they are already at lower multiples.

It appears now that the average multiple (stock price to earnings) should be adjusted downward at least temporarily and perhaps permanently, due to the reckless use of leverage over the last several decades. Therefore, our outlook is for multiple compressions. Stocks could hit their earnings targets, but still be worth less—but not worthless, by any means.

Fixed Income, Interest Rates, and Inflation

Traditionally, there has been a relationship between fixed income yields and economic growth. Recently, that relationship has not been normal due to the aggressive actions taken by the Fed to address the recession and the need to stabilize the economy. Looking ahead, it is likely that this relationship will "normalize," thereby sending short-term rates slightly higher.

To explain, there is a relationship between economic growth and interest rates, with the two-year interest rate, on average, tending to equal four quarters' average GDP growth. When an interest rate slips to negative, one would typically assume that GDP is also going to drop into negative territory. Currently, with a slight tick up in inflation, real yields are negative (nominal rate minus inflation equals the real yield). However, even with my somewhat pessimistic view, I do not foresee economic growth slipping to levels that equal the real rate.

The reason is that the relationship between fixed income yields and the economy is not following normal patterns. While real rates have slipped into negative territory, we think that indicates the economy is going to slow down, but not to the point of going to a negative rate. Therefore, for the relationship to normalize, rates need to be higher.

Meanwhile, although inflation did pick up in 2011, without widespread employment gains and wage increases it would be difficult to support sustained higher levels of inflation that would further make the real yield lower as well. Thus, while I expect yields to normalize (read: be slightly higher) even in the face of a weakening economy, I don't expect inflation to get out of hand.

Interestingly, the Fed recently announced that it is going to provide clearer forecasts of where its rate policies are headed. As the Fed becomes much more transparent to the point of telegraphing where rates are going, I would listen more closely to those pronouncements. This has been a significant change in Fed behavior and the days of trying to discern the meaning of tersely worded statements. (Next thing you know, the Fed governors will be on "The View" and making the rounds to Letterman and Leno, as well.) Bottom line: when the Fed speaks, listen.

The Dollar, Commodities, and Energy

The U.S. dollar ended 2011 slightly higher from where it began. Although that may not look monumental, consider that the widespread view last year was for the dollar to fall on hard times. A year ago, we said we expected the "underdog" dollar to continue to surprise on the upside—and it did. As we look at 2012, we are more bullish than bearish on the dollar, and do not expect the greenback to lose its status as the preferred currency any time soon, with the objective of it being more stable in the years ahead.

As for commodities, they gained a lot of attention over the past few years. From corn to copper, commodities captured everyone's eye. Now they are on the back burner again, garnering much less attention. What happens in energy, meanwhile, will be a function of global growth. The solution for higher energy prices is, simply, higher energy prices. When prices go higher, alternative supplies become more viable, which increases supply. And, higher prices cut consumption, which decreases demand. Higher supply and lower demand equal lower prices. With the forecast for subpar growth, energy may trend higher, but I am not overly concerned.

Real Estate and Housing

A big question mark hung over the housing market in 2011, although there were certainly opportunities for private investors and those who wished to buy real estate stocks. Our advice a year ago was to be certain of what you're buying before you make a move (which is good advice for anything these days). In the residential market, a supply overhang remains problematic, although things have been improving slowly.

We are not out of the woods yet with housing; we are still in the process of putting in the trough. The good news, as we said last year, is that we do not need housing to turn around for the economy to be okay. For the economy to have a sustained, vibrant growth trajectory, yes, housing needs to strengthen. But the current level of housing, both prices and transactions, can support a flat economy. Therefore, the housing market as it now stands won't be a problem. Over time, economics will likely be the solution to the housing market as the population transitions from buying to renting. Then, at some point, the trend will reverse, and the economic viability of buying versus renting will help support housing prices.

Conclusion: The Year of Zero

It appears 2012 is setting up to be what I call an inside year; by that I mean the close of the year will be somewhere in the range of 2011. While we might breach the extremes of 2011 temporarily, it doesn't appear that any good news can sustain the upside, while even the headwinds from high debt levels, weak demand, and global political drama won't be able to hold the valuations much lower than the 2011 lows.

The U.S. economy and the global economy were seriously damaged by the 2008 financial crisis. The crisis itself was the result of behaviors that over many years created a fragile economy that could not sustain itself without serious adjustments. Although this is not the forum for me to get on my soapbox about all the political, social, and economic changes that need to be made, suffice it to say that adjustments are needed. While these transitions are underway, the outlook for 2012 appears benign.

Specifically for the year, debt levels must be lower in both the private and public sector. This will cause GDP to slow and job growth to moderate. Earnings are still likely to grow, albeit at lower than last year's pace; however, multiples will contract, offsetting earnings growth. Thus, 2012 is the year of the zero.

Over the last few decades we've seen increased volatility, including in the housing market. Extreme gyrations (which create the left and right tails on the normal distribution of price action over time) are not typical. Therefore, one of the objectives of the Fed policies, it appears, has been to take the tails out of it (meaning the extreme moves up and down), which given the flat year of 2011, shows this thinking in action.

I would expect volatility to narrow so that investors have a much more definable space for their investments (in other words, don't expect to make or lose 50 percent in any given market). Yes, stocks and bonds will move and might move against you at times. But you won't have to worry about having your head handed to you. It's also apparent that the Fed has been concerned about a fixed-income bubble; thus some of its policies are aimed at shifting investors slowly away from those instruments. This underscores our belief that 2012 will be the year of zero as the Fed policies reduce risk. When risk is reduced, so is return.

Although 2012 as the year of the zero may sound boring or even disappointing, we can't deny that under the circumstances and compared to where many people thought we would be three years ago this is not so bad. Up five percent or down five percent is meaningless, not much more than a rounding error compared to the cliff we were hanging over just a few years ago. The good news is we didn't fall. The initial rebound was obvious; a dead cat bounces after all. The next leg up was impressive as growth was weak and challenges abound globally. Staying solvent and within a five percent point range on both sides of zero tells a much bigger story than many have been hearing. We survived! Looking at the data for 2012, I still see challenges ahead and market dislocations, but we have a market and economy that still function. That is good news, indeed. Everything else is actually moot.

Chapter 3

RISK, REWARD, AND TRUE DIVERSIFICATION WITH ETFS

True diversification with active management focuses on the overall market and the economy rather than individual stocks and bonds.

If you said the word "diversification" to most retail investors, what would their response be? Most likely they would say that diversification is achieved by holding a certain percentage of assets in stocks and a certain percentage in fixed income. Or, they might take it a step further and suggest that to diversify within an asset class, such as stocks, you need to hold a variety of equities: large cap, mid cap, small cap, growth, value, etc. Although these beliefs are widely held among retail investors, they are not examples of true diversification. To use a simple analogy, it's like filling up a dish with a scoop of vanilla, another of chocolate, a third of strawberry, and a fourth of pistachio, and maybe a few scoops of rocky road and mint-chocolate chip. It may look and taste different, but it's still ice cream, and you haven't achieved a balanced diet just by mixing the colors and a few flavors on your plate. And if you leave it out too long, it will all melt into an indistinguishable mess.

Similarly, as investment professionals and savvy investors know all too well, holding different kinds of stock will not provide true diversification, particularly in market downturns. In a bear market, some stocks will be quicker to fall than others. For example, the small cap growth stocks may get hit first, while the more conservative large cap value issues hold up a little better. But in time, most equities will go down. The only variation is the degree to which they decline. So, if one type of stock goes down 10 percent, another stock declines 25 percent, and yet another drops 50 percent, is that diversification within equities? I don't think so.

Active management is a highly effective way to achieve true diversification within equities, or any other asset class for that matter. With an active management approach to equities, investors can buy (go long) when economic indicators point to an expansion and the stock market is rising. Conversely, investors can sell to exit long positions in equities (or even go short) when economic indicators point to a contraction and the stock market is falling.

Economics-Based Active Management

ECONOMIC EXPANSION: Favors buying equities (long).

ECONOMIC CONTRACTION: Favors selling equities (taking profits or establishing short position), increasing cash and fixed income.

LONG OR SHORT: Broad market exposure through exchange-traded funds (ETFs) that replicate major indices such as S&P 500 and Nasdaq 100.

Understanding Active Management

True diversification is achieved through a long/short active management strategy. Active management means taking a proactive approach to investing by utilizing fundamental and/or technical analysis to create value in a portfolio beyond buy-and-hold. In fact, active management is the antithesis of buy-and-hold investing.

As stated previously, the economy has cycles (expansion, peak, contraction, and trough) just like a year has its seasons. Throughout the economic cycles, the market goes up and goes down. The key is to address these cycles and add value to a portfolio by providing strategies that work in all market conditions. Given recent events in the market, more investors than ever are looking for ways to mitigate losses in adverse market conditions and even to create profitable opportunities in bear markets.

At Astor, we have developed strategies that position client portfolios to profit in both up and down markets, through all the aforementioned cycles. Our programs work to diversify portfolios so that the drawdowns that investors typically experience during down markets are not as deep, while still helping accounts to grow during up markets.

 For investors who want to achieve true diversification through bullish and bearish cycles in the market, active management is the key. And the instruments that can best help you to accomplish that are exchange-traded funds (ETFs).

The Investment Process Using ETFs

When investors want to gain exposure to the stock market, often they choose a mutual fund or a stock that they like. Any number of criteria can trigger their decisions, from advertisements to something they heard from someone else. I would argue that the best way to gain exposure to the stock market is through a product called the exchange-traded fund, or ETF. An ETF is a collection of securities that tracks, or is intended to represent, the performance of either a broad or specific segment of the market. For example, if you wanted exposure to the S&P 500, you could choose the SPDR S&P 500 ETF, nicknamed the "spider," which trades under the symbol SPY. For something more specialized such as biotechnology, you could choose a more narrowly focused ETF, such as the SPDR S&P Biotech (XBI) or PowerShares Dynamic Biotech and Genome Portfolio (PBE). With ETFs, you can make an investment in a broad index or a sector simply by buying shares, such as you would in your favorite company.

Astor constructs portfolios using ETFs. These instruments are a pure play on a specific index or sector. The transparency and low expenses of ETFs make them ideal investment choices for Astor's macroeconomic approach. Further, there is a vast range of ETFs available, covering multiple asset classes, sectors, and investment styles beyond the broad indexes such as the S&P 500, Nasdaq 100, and Dow Jones Industrial Average. Using ETFs, portfolios can be constructed that offer true diversification across various asset classes and in all types of market conditions.

The ETF Advantage

LOW COST: ETFs typically have low management fees and expense ratios because they require less active management than mutual funds. Most ETFs are designed to track a benchmark, which can mean fewer trades and lower portfolio turnover.

TAX EFFICIENCY: Since ETFs are passively managed, they usually realize fewer capital gains than actively managed funds. This reduces the frequency of tax gain distributions.

TRANSPARENT: ETFs provide investors with the required information to make informed investment decisions. Investors have access to all securities held within an ETF on a daily basis.

ALL-DAY ACCESS: ETFs trade throughout the day, enabling investors to lock in the market value of an ETF at any time during the trading day. Investors can enter or exit a position when they want, not just the end of the day, as with mutual funds.

VAST EXPOSURE: ETFs provide exposure to asset classes which, until recently, were off-limits to the average investor.

Avoiding Catastrophe

At one time it was unfathomable: a well-established company that suddenly was trading for only a few dollars per share—or less. Consider Ford Motor Company that dropped below $2.00 per share in 2009, after trading around $30 in 2001. Or consider Bear Stearns, which in 2007 was trading above $150 a share and was sold in 2008 for $10 a share after the firm nearly failed. When Lehman Brothers went bankrupt in the fall of 2008, shareholders were wiped out. As these examples show, the risk of being in the wrong stock at the wrong time is huge. With ETFs, however, the risk of going to zero is nil. Yes, an ETF can see a downward move of 20 percent or more, but the chance of going to zero is remote, if not mathematically impossible. The reason is that ETFs are made up of dozens, and sometimes even hundreds, of stocks. Therefore, even if you have a few big losers in the index, the ETF will not go to zero. During the financial crisis, for example, the Financial Select Sector SPDR (XLF) was down 30 percent or so at one point, but was still a far better investment than the likes of Lehman Brothers or Bear Stearns. Granted, having an ETF lose a third of its value is painful, but it's not a complete washout.

There are numerous ETFs, from those that track metals and other commodities to others that offer exposure to emerging markets or fixed income. There are even inverse ETFs that allow you to replicate a short position in a particular index. Buying inverse instruments, which go up in value when the underlying index goes down, allows you to hedge your portfolio. An investor could even construct a no-risk portfolio of longs and shorts using ETFs, with the security of knowing that positions could be liquidated at any time.

Praise for the ETF

I am on record as saying that the ETF is the greatest financial innovation since the creation of the put! To understand why I feel so strongly about these instruments, allow me to explain. Back in the early days of options, there were only calls, which gave the buyer the right, but not the obligation, to take a long position in the underlying security. Calls worked great if you thought the market was going up, but if you wanted a short position you were basically out of luck. Writing calls (meaning to sell them) would have given you short exposure, but with far too much risk exposure. With the creation of the put, it became possible to establish a short position by buying an option. When you buy a put, you have the opportunity, but not the obligation, to be short the market, and the only thing you stand to lose is the premium you paid.

ETFs, in my opinion, give investors the same flexibility: establishing long and short positions easily by buying an instrument—and without the complexity of shorting a stock. In addition, specialized ETFs allow investors to be long or short a particular sector or industry.

For Astor, using ETFs to construct our portfolios allows us to put our economic strategy into action. As explained in Chapter 1, during an economic expansion phase, the objective is to be long the broad market, such as the S&P or the Dow, which can be easily accomplished using ETFs. In addition, we may want to use specialized ETFs to gain exposure to a particular sector that is doing well and outpacing the growth of the overall economy. Whatever my investment hypothesis, there are ETFs that allow me to put my ideas into action.

As I have stated, I do not believe stock picking is an efficient way to invest, particularly for the average individual. The expertise I have developed and honed over the years is analyzing the economy to identify the current economic phase (expansion, peak, contraction, or trough) and then to invest accordingly. I prefer a long-term horizon and making investment decisions based on particular economic fundamentals. Plus, taking a sector approach avoids the risk of being invested in the wrong stock. Even if you correctly identify the market trend and pick a strong sector, you could still choose the wrong stock, whether it's one that lags because of a poor performing business unit or other fundamental problems. With an ETF, you gain sector exposure across multiple stocks. Using ETFs to invest, however, does mean that you won't get the sky-high returns of the rare stock whose gains outpace all other issues in a sector. But unless you are a professional stock analyst, your chance of accomplishing that is akin to finding a diamond on the beach. A far more prudent strategy is to use ETFs to gain exposure to the broad market and specific sectors.

Whether the overall trend is bullish or bearish, it is important to distinguish between the broad market and individual sectors. Even during 2008, when the stock market's performance was absolutely dismal, there were a few bright spots; among them, transportation. The lesson here is to look beyond your normal benchmarks such as the Dow when you are building a portfolio. Even if the entire market is down that does not mean there will not be sectors that are performing well, or that when the market rallies some sectors will outperform the rest.

Investing with ETFs allows you to think like an economist, instead of trying to be a stock picker. Your investment decisions are based on what you see happening in the economy and in particular sectors. This is a good approach no matter which way the wind blows in the future.

Active Management Scenarios

Now, let's review a few scenarios in which active management plays a part. At Astor, our goal is to use true diversification to achieve less volatile long-term capital appreciation and lower drawdowns, thereby attempting to generate a more stable risk/return curve than our benchmark.

First, I want to emphasize that it is not the role of the asset manager, the professional who is actively managing a portfolio, to determine an individual's risk tolerance and market exposure. That decision is best made by the client, with input from his or her investment advisor, based on factors such as the investor's age, investment time horizon, earnings power, overall holdings, and risk tolerance. For example, if a client has no appetite for risk, as evidenced by a large percentage of holdings in fixed-income assets, this individual is not a good candidate for active management. If equities were a small percentage of the person's overall portfolio, then the active management portion of those holdings would be similarly confined to a small percentage.

If someone has moderate risk tolerance, with roughly half of his or her portfolio in equities and half in fixed income, then at least half of the person's equity assets (or 25 percent of the overall portfolio) would be invested in an active management program. This approach significantly reduces the risk of the long-only equity approach of the portfolio during market downturns. Moreover, this approach also increases the potential return over time.

To illustrate this point, consider this scenario: An investor holds 100 percent of her portfolio in equities. If the market declines by 10 percent over time, the equity holdings would also be down about 10 percent, plus or minus a few percentage points, depending upon the performance of the individual stocks in her portfolio. However, if half of the portfolio were invested using an active management approach, then sometime during the market's decline, the investor would have at least exited the market. Or, if her risk tolerance allowed it, she would be short the market with half of her overall equity holdings. Thus, during the downturn, her losses would be at least cut in half compared to what they would be if she continued to hold her entire equity portfolio. With a short position, she could reap profits during a downturn that would offset losses on her equities, possibly to the extent that she broke even or made a small profit. In the worst-case scenario, she would have a smaller drawdown than with a full equity exposure and in the best case she would realize a modest profit.

Now, when the market turns and begins to recover, the investor can fully invest in equities again. But instead of having to make up for a 10 percent decline in her entire portfolio, she is starting off with a small loss, a breakeven position, or a small profit. When the expanding market increases the value of the stocks in her portfolio, the investor reaps a larger return over time—and, more important, with reduced risk.

Model Portfolios

With this understanding, let's take a look at some hypothetical investor scenarios, and how active management could be used to reduce risk and enhance returns. In each instance, the risk tolerance determination from a portfolio management perspective is based on the percentage of equities held in an individual investor's portfolio.

Jonathan, a 36-year-old professional, is an aggressive investor whose portfolio is 90 percent invested in equities with ten percent held in lower risk fixed income. Given his equity exposure and risk tolerance, Jonathan hopes to make large gains during a bull market. During market downturns, however, Jonathan stands potentially to lose a significant portion of his portfolio value. This is the underlying problem with equity portfolios. The inevitable downturns in the stock market often occur when an equity-based portfolio is at the peak of its worth.

For Jonathan, the investment recommendation would be for about half of his equity holdings to be actively managed. Specifically, I would recommend about half of his equity holdings to be managed with a long/short strategy. The essence of the long/short strategy is to be long equities when the economic indicators confirm an expansion, and to be short equities during a contraction. Let's take a look at Jonathan's portfolio during each stage of the economic or business cycle:

Expansion Mode: Jonathan

During economic expansion—as evidenced by GDP growth, relatively low unemployment, and an appreciating stock market—Jonathan will be heavily invested in equities. In keeping with his risk tolerance and investment temperament, during an expansion Jonathan's holdings will be 90 percent equities, but in a very specific mix:

Jonathan's Model Portfolio: Expansion	
Total Equity Holdings	Total Fixed-Income and Cash Equivalents
90%	10%
45% - Individual Stocks	
45% - Active Management Equity (Indices) Holdings	

To reap the benefits of broad exposure to the stock market during an economic expansion, 45 percent of his equity holdings will be actively managed using ETFs that replicate exposure to stock indices; specifically, the S&P 500 and Nasdaq 100.

Although Jonathan is an aggressive investor with 90 percent of his overall holdings in equities, we would not recommend more than 50 to 60 percent of those holdings being actively managed. The prime consideration is to use active management as a strategy to meaningfully diversify a portfolio, not to dominate or overwhelm it. Through active management, his equity holdings can be enhanced, while offering profit protection and opportunities to reap further gains during market contractions.

For an aggressive investor such as Jonathan, another component of active management may also be included. A portion of his actively managed investment will be deployed in a momentum and trend-following system. This active entry/exit strategy would allow Jonathan to benefit from opportunities—both short and long—that arise during the prevailing trend.

The objective of the active entry/exit strategy is to buy and sell, depending upon momentum and trend indicators, to take advantage of relatively short-term market moves. Several indicators can be used as part of the active entry/exit strategy. By capturing these moves, which occur frequently within a longer-term trend, returns can be further enhanced and risk can be reduced.

The most important consideration is to be disciplined in this approach, and to use only a portion of the actively managed assets. That way, even if a short-term directional move is missed, the majority of the assets that are actively managed remain invested according to the longer-term economic trend.

To illustrate how the positioning of Jonathan's portfolio would work, let's assume that now the economy starts to deteriorate. Long positions in the actively managed portion of his equity portfolio would be exited. If the market were down 50+ percent, active management could limit Jonathan's loss; for example, to 10 to 15 percent. When the market rebounds and Jonathan re-enters his stock positions, it will take far less of an up move to get him back to flat; for example, a 7.5 percent stock market rise would erase about a 13 to 15 percent portfolio decline.

In contrast, a buy-and-hold investor would have been down significantly more at the bottom of the market's decline, and even after a partial rebound would still be down considerably. Not only does Jonathan end up with a better performance, compared with a loss for the buy-and-hold investor, but he also does so with fewer of what I call "ulcer points." In other words, by actively managing his portfolio, he can reduce his risk in adverse market conditions easily and efficiently, while reaping the rewards of following the market trends, as defined by economic data. Similar results can also be achieved by actively managing assets in other markets as well, including fixed income, from both a short and long perspective.

Contraction Mode: Jonathan

During an economic contraction—as evidenced by a decline in the GDP rate, increasing unemployment, and a decline in the stock market—active management would seek to protect Jonathan's gains that were reaped during the expansion phase. Beyond taking profits and selling a portion of his equity holdings, active management would also seek to profit through short positions during the contraction. This is achieved by establishing outright short positions replicated using inverse ETFs.

Outside of the actively managed portion of the portfolio, Jonathan and his investment advisor could also decide to sell some individual stocks and increase his fixed-income and cash-equivalent holdings. For the sake of this illustration, we will assume that Jonathan decides to reduce his individual stock holdings and increase his fixed income/cash equivalents as shown. His actively managed portion, however, remains approximately 45 percent of his previous overall equity holdings.

Jonathan's Model Portfolio: Contraction

Total Equity Holdings	Total Fixed Income and Cash Equivalents
90% (before adjustment)	10%
25% - Individual Stocks	30%
45% - Active Management Equity Holdings	

The actively managed portion of his equity holdings would utilize inverse ETFs to establish a short position in the indices. (Remember, the value of an inverse ETF increases when the underlying index declines.) The objective of active management during the contraction is two-fold. First, it lessens Jonathan's long equity exposure during the unfavorable market conditions associated with a contraction. Second, it seeks to reap profits from the falling market, which could at least offset losses Jonathan incurs elsewhere in his portfolio. Potentially, if his short position is sizeable enough and the market decline is significant, Jonathan could make a net profit on his overall holdings.

In addition, the active entry/exit strategy would be utilized to capitalize on short-term momentum and trend opportunities. Again, this would involve about 20 percent of Jonathan's actively managed holdings. The objective would be to look for opportunities to buy the market to take advantage of short-term, upward countertrend moves that occur during contractions and to sell when the move is over.

Throughout the management of Jonathan's holdings, the strategies deployed match his investment objectives, time frame, and risk tolerance. This is far better than determining an individual's holdings based upon age alone, which assumes that every 30-year-old, 50-year-old, or 70-year-old has the same risk tolerance and time frame. There could be risk-averse 30-year-olds for whom active management should be deployed conservatively, if at all. Or, there could be highly risk tolerant

70-year-olds for whom active management would be an ideal strategy. Once again, it is the role of the investment advisor, who knows the clients best, to advise them.

Expansion Mode: Monica

Monica is a 59-year-old widow with two grown children. A moderate-risk investor, she has roughly half of her holdings in equities and half in fixed income or cash equivalents. Her investment objective is to preserve capital while also growing her portfolio steadily over time. Active management within her equity holdings will help further these goals.

During economic expansion, Monica's overall holdings will reflect her 50/50 split. However, the equity portion will be divided between individual stocks and active management holdings, using a long/short strategy.

Monica's Model Portfolio: Expansion	
Total Equity Holdings	Total Fixed Income and Cash Equivalents
50%	50%
25% - Individual Stocks	
25% - Active Management Equity Holdings	

As in the previous example, the actively managed portion will utilize ETFs to replicate long exposure to the S&P 500 and Nasdaq 100. Although Monica is a moderate-risk investor, we would not recommend less than 50 percent of her equity holdings be deployed using active management, representing 25 percent of her overall portfolio. If a smaller percentage were committed to active management, the overall diversification effect would be greatly diluted.

Using the long/short strategy, Monica would have long exposure to the major indices when the economic data indicated that expansion was continuing. Because of her overall moderate risk tolerance and her need for capital preservation, the more aggressive, active entry/exit strategy would not be deployed.

Contraction Mode: Monica

During economic contraction, Monica's equity position could remain at 50 percent of her portfolio or at a slightly smaller percentage if she and her investment advisor decide to sell some individual stocks in her portfolio. Nonetheless, 25 percent of her portfolio would continue to be actively managed. In this scenario, a slight adjustment to her equity holdings is assumed.

Monica's Model Portfolio: Contraction

Total Equity Holdings	Total Fixed Income and Cash Equivalents
45%	55%

20% - Individual Stocks
25% - Active Management Equity Holdings

In keeping with the long/short strategy deployed for her actively managed holdings, short positions would be established using ETFs as soon as an economic contraction was detected and confirmed. Throughout the economic contraction, this portion of her portfolio would remain short to capitalize on the overall downtrend. The goal would be to offset losses incurred from her other equity holdings, thus preserving capital and providing a better foundation for the future when the economy turned and expansion resumed.

Although active management can be deployed to reduce risk and potentially improve returns, it is not for every investor. For example, Donald and Sylvia are in their mid-50s. Their portfolio is held mostly in 401(k) and other retirement holdings. They are conservative investors with about 70 percent of their holdings in fixed income and cash equivalents and 30 percent in equities, mostly mutual funds. Given their low risk tolerance, active management would not be an appropriate strategy for them. In fact, an investment professional who knows this couple and their risk tolerance would not even present active management to them.

As these model portfolios illustrate, true asset diversification can maximize returns and minimize overall risk, by taking advantage of opportunities presented in rising and falling markets. Most important, the strategies must be tailored to the individual's investment objectives and risk tolerance. In fact, that is the beauty of active management. When the optimal portion of a portfolio is committed to an active management strategy, an investor can protect against adverse market moves without putting too much of his or her holdings at risk. Active management is a powerful strategy that belongs in many investors' portfolios.

The key is for investors to work with their advisors to determine the right portfolio mix to match their risk profile, while pursuing their objectives for growth and capital preservation.

Chapter 4

ACTIVE MANAGEMENT A VALUE PROPOSITION

Getting the economic direction correct is not only a good predictor for market performance over months or years, but it also makes it much easier to predict the outcome from surprise events.

Over the long-term, the average annual return from owning stocks historically has been just under 10 percent. (According to Jeremy Siegel, author of *Stocks for the Long Run*, between 1886 and 2001, historic returns averaged about 9.76 percent per year.) That is not a bad annual return if you can realize it, but most funds underperform their benchmark indexes on a regular basis. Moreover, even if you were able to achieve an average annual return of 9.76 percent, buy-and-hold has an inherent problem as a stand-alone strategy. On your way to achieving that target return, you could see your capital decline by 30 to 60 percent at times—and typically when you have the largest exposure to the markets. Further, as fate would have it, your portfolio could very well decline when you need your money most.

We are, by nature, emotional beings, and sitting through these stomach-churning market episodes is very difficult to do. In fact, most investors end up selling near the bottom and do not get back in until the market is well past the previous exit point on the way back up. With that action alone, you miss a significant portion of the market's return and need to work even harder to get it back. In other words, you have to sit through a 30 to 60 percent pullback only to achieve a long-term average return of less than 10 percent (if you did, indeed, sit through it).

Keep in mind that 9.76 percent is a simple arithmetic average return. Actual returns, geometrically stated (taking into account compounding), could be significantly less.

Some investors do hold through the ups and downs, attempting to weather the storm, because they have a longer time horizon for their financial needs. But what would happen if one of those financial needs occurred sooner than expected, or something came up and you needed money now? If that need arose in the middle or, worse yet, at the bottom of the drawdown (see years seven or eight in Figure 4.1), how devastating could that be? Aside from the financial need to make up a greater portion of those assets, it also reduces the capital base from which to compound your returns during the next positive period.

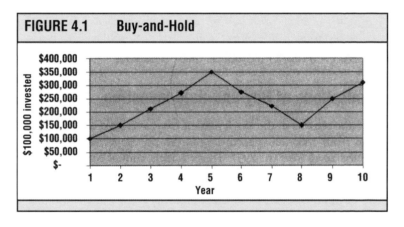

FIGURE 4.1   Buy-and-Hold

What is missing in most investment portfolios is a strategy that smoothes out the impact of adverse market conditions. There is, however, a value-added strategy that can limit your drawdowns without sacrificing your upside potential. This value-added strategy is called active management, as illustrated in the hypothetical example shown in Figure 4.2. In this scenario, you would have a much easier time (and less worry) meeting financial demands in years seven and eight. The bottom line is that active management allows you to make financial decisions on your own terms, not the market's terms.

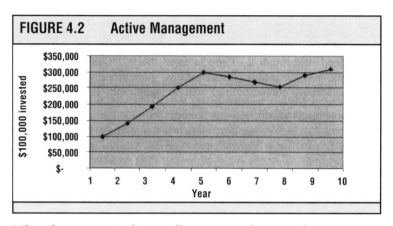

FIGURE 4.2   Active Management

When the economy is doing well, you can make money by investing in almost any sector. But that is not where the real value of active management lies. When the economy is doing poorly, however, you can lose money in almost any sector. An active management strategy responds to changes in the economy and positions you to limit the losses. Now that is value!

To further illustrate the purpose of using active management to achieve true diversification, we created a hypothetical portfolio containing just stocks and bonds. We then compared that to what the same portfolio may have looked like had you used an active management approach, such as Astor's, in your portfolio during that same time period.

Figure 4.3 shows the results of a hypothetical, moderately conservative buy-and-hold portfolio (the lighter line), which contained a 60 percent allocation to the S&P 500 (an unmanaged composite of 500 large capitalization companies) and a 40 percent allocation to the Barclays Capital Aggregate Bond Index (a composite return of a diverse range of U.S. debt instruments, previously known as the Lehman Brothers Aggregate Bond Index). The active management model (the darker line) was comprised of 100 percent equities (S&P 500) during economic expansion and 100 percent fixed income (Barclays bond index) during economic contractions or recession.

During the period of economic growth from 2005 to 2007, the active management model portfolio produced returns that closely tracked the hypothetical buy-and-hold 60/40 investor portfolio. During the

2008 to 2009 recession (the darker shade on the timeline), however, the divergence between the two portfolios shows the real value-added of active management. A defensive position of 100 percent fixed income during the recession stabilized the active management portfolio and established a higher base from which to grow after the recession ended and the economy began expanding again.

The active management model was able to significantly outperform the straight buy-and-hold, as it was able to sidestep the decline and position the portfolio to garner returns during the economic contraction. As you can imagine, a more aggressive buy-and-hold portfolio (one containing higher beta stocks with less fixed income) would have seen more pronounced drawdowns, particularly during 2008 to 2009.

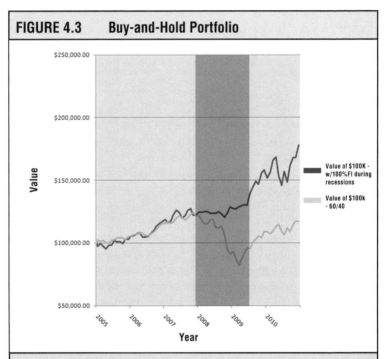

FIGURE 4.3   Buy-and-Hold Portfolio

Comparison of a conservative buy-and-hold portfolio of 60 percent equities and 40 percent bonds (lighter line) with active management model (darker line). The real value of the active management approach is clearly visible during and after the 2008 to 2009 economic contraction and recession.

Risk and Reward

The greater the risk investors are willing to take, the greater the potential reward they are going to require in return for that risk. Standard deviation is one measure of risk or volatility of a certain asset. (Treasury yields are labeled as risk-free assets because the risk of default or non-payment on the coupon and principal is minimal.) Generally speaking, in order to reduce risk, you end up sacrificing return. However, active management has the unique ability to diminish overall risk without reducing long-term returns, as you can see in Figure 4.4.

Figure 4.4   Risk/Return

	Buy and Hold			Mix		
	Return	Std. Dev.	Return to Risk Ratio	Return	Std. Dev.	Return to Risk Ratio
1 year	34.51%	9.69%	3.56	40.59%	5.77%	7.03
3 year	1.42%	15.45%	0.09	5.08%	10.44%	0.49
5 year	1.69%	12.05%	0.14	6.24%	8.41%	0.74
10 Year	2.01%	11.38%	0.18	3.41%	9.52%	0.36

Comparison of buy-and-hold portfolio (60 percent equities and 40 percent fixed income) with an active management mix. Half of the mix portfolio is invested in S&P 500 (60 percent) and half in Barclays Capital Aggregate Bond Index (40 percent). The other half of the mixed portfolio is invested with 100 percent equities (S&P 500) during economic expansion and 100 percent fixed income (Barclays index) during contractions. As Figure 4.4 shows, the mixed portfolio has a higher return-to-risk ratio compared to buy-and-hold.

Why You Should Worry About Drawdowns

One of the most important considerations when choosing an investment is the amount of drawdown you will likely experience and how long it would take to recover.

- **Drawdown:** The total decrease (percentage or dollars) that your account falls from the highest peak value achieved in the account.

- **Recovery**: How long it takes from the low value in the drawdown to get back to new highs.

The results in Figure 4.5 show the drawdown and recovery during a classic example: the period of 2001 to 2003. The results illustrate the importance of reducing drawdowns, which shortens recovery time.

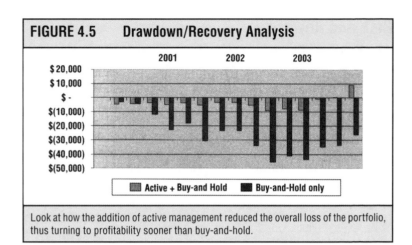

FIGURE 4.5   Drawdown/Recovery Analysis

Look at how the addition of active management reduced the overall loss of the portfolio, thus turning to profitability sooner than buy-and-hold.

If we have failed to drive the idea home at this point, consider the following: hypothetically, if you invested your money during the second quarter of 2000 (the worst possible time within the historic snapshot shown in Figure 4.5) you would have realized the following cumulative gains/losses during the corresponding quarters. Your buy-and-hold portfolio, if mixed with active management, would have lost no more than $9,200, compared with a loss of $46,000 in an S&P 500 buy-and-hold position. Additionally, the active mix portfolio would have already recovered and posted a gain of more than $8,500 while the buy-and-hold portfolio was still down $25,000, even with a 30 percent-plus return in 2003.

The Case Study

Figure 4.6 depicts a more aggressive, all-equity buy-and-hold portfolio (the lighter line on the chart) that correlated 100 percent with the S&P 500 for the time period shown. When the economic contraction and recession of 2008 to 2009 hit (the shaded area on the timeline) the buy-and-hold portfolio suffered significant losses. Recovery from these losses will take a considerable amount of time and percentage gains. In contrast, the active management model (the darker line) switches to a defensive position of fixed income-only during the contraction and recession, thus guarding against losses and positioning the portfolio for growth when the economy begins expanding again.

As Figure 4.6 shows, the major benefit of active management occurs during uncertain or changing market conditions. With a significant reduction in volatility in the value of your assets, you can feel more comfortable making important financial decisions, and have a larger asset base to compound during positive market environments.

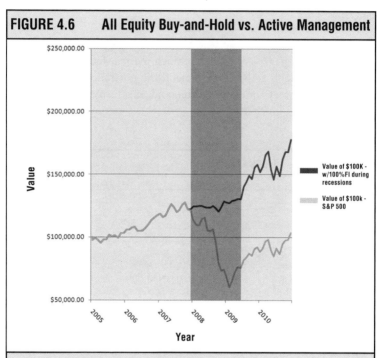

FIGURE 4.6   All Equity Buy-and-Hold vs. Active Management

Comparison of buy-and-hold/equity-only portfolio with an active management model, which switches to a 100 percent fixed income position during economic contractions or recession.

Conclusion

The deeper the declines in your portfolio, the greater the returns you will need in subsequent periods to restore the initial value of your portfolio. If a portfolio of $100,000 declines by 50 percent to $50,000, you will need a 100 percent return from that point to recover the initial value. If you are able to cut that loss to 25 percent to a lowest portfolio value of $75,000, that portfolio will need only a 33 percent return from that point to recover the initial value. All else being equal, the 33 percent return should take significantly less time to achieve than the 100 percent, based on the laws of positive compounding (which are much more effective following limited drawdowns). We all know that time is one of the most important factors in investing that we can have on our side.

The points made in the case study are clear in Figure 4.7. The addition of active management created a much more desirable effect in the long term. Through active management, the portfolio drawdown was smaller, the recovery time was shorter, and, as a result, overall returns were greater with much less risk.

Figure 4.7   Less Losses

	Buy - And- Hold	Active Mix
Beginning Investment	$100,000.00	$100,000.00
Lowest value of account during period	$81,908.16	$98,022.68
Largest yearly return during period	9.63%	10.05%
Current Value (2010)	$117,052.30	$142,002.96
Out-performance of buy-and-hold by mix		21.32%

Comparison of buy-and-hold portfolio with the active management model mix. Although the active mix does post a larger yearly return during the period 2000 to 2010, the more important data point is the lowest value of the account during the period. Active management lost less than $2,000, while the buy-and-hold portfolio declined by more than $18,000.

Summary: Strategies for Tomorrow's Markets

Market corrections of the past have taught us an important albeit painful lesson, one that we at Astor have been teaching clients for years. Rather than putting their hopes (and money) on buy-and-hold, investors must recognize the need to take a more active approach to investing. To meet the needs of these sophisticated investors, investment professionals should offer more than just the mutual fund flavor of the month or hot stock pick. Savvy investors are looking for strategies that will serve them not only in today's market conditions, but tomorrow's as well.

To meet the needs of their clients, investment professionals must understand the advantages of active management, which allows investment decisions to be made based on specific market conditions and other criteria, such as Astor's strategy of economics-based active management.

Through active management, investors have the potential to improve returns and reduce risk. Moreover, they can bring true diversification to their portfolios to guard against downturns and improve returns in favorable conditions. This is vitally important in today's new investment climate of shorter, less defined cycles.

Bullish or bearish, economic expansion or contraction, the cycles will continue. Savvy investors and the investment professionals who advise them should not be afraid when the cycles change. Through active management, they will be empowered to make bolder decisions which, over time, can improve returns while reducing unfavorable market exposure.

ABOUT ASTOR ASSET MANAGEMENT

▲ ▲ ▲ ▲ ▲ ▲

Astor Asset Management is an SEC-registered investment firm and subsidiary of Knight Capital Group, Inc. (NYSE Euronext: KCG). Founded in 2001 by Rob Stein, Astor offers actively-managed portfolios of ETFs to protect and grow capital over time by pursuing an attractive absolute compounded return without the performance fees and lock-up periods associated with hedge funds.

Astor manages over $1.2 billion in assets and its portfolios are available through most financial brokerage firms in both separately managed accounts and mutual funds. The firm uses a proprietary macroeconomic model and tactical strategies to create a diversified portfolio of non-correlating ETFs within all asset classes (equities, fixed income, commodities, currencies, REITs).

The Astor Advantage

Astor seeks to generate positive returns in both up and down markets (an absolute return approach). During market expansions, it utilizes diversified, non-correlating long equity ETF positions. During economic contractions, the portfolios will utilize defensive positioning, which can range from overweighting cash and fixed income to using ETFs with inverse exposure to broad market averages. The goal is to create a positively-sloped return curve that will benefit from the direction of the economic trend.

Astor Asset Management believes that long-term financial goals for investors are capital appreciation, limited volatility, and quick recovery time from market losses. The firm's view is that these goals can be achieved by diversifying investments among various asset classes and employing the use of low-cost investment products within an overall portfolio. Astor seeks to limit drawdowns and generate profits in virtually all market environments. The basis of our philosophy is identifying the recurring economic cycles of expansion, peak, contraction, and trough, and actively rebalancing when the cycles change.

Astor's proprietary macroeconomic model analyzes economic data such as GDP, inflation, employment, money flows, and overall market conditions to determine the current phase of the business cycle (expansion, peak, contraction, or trough). Once the current phase of the business cycle is identified, Astor, through active management, rebalances its portfolios. Active rebalancing occurs only when the economic cycle changes.

By analyzing macroeconomic factors, our goal is to achieve a less volatile return and higher return-to-risk-ratio than our benchmark. Tactical asset allocation is utilized to create exposure to a variety of market sectors, capitalizations, and styles. Our objective is to produce positive returns, not necessarily to outperform a benchmark. For more information about Astor, or to contact Robert N. Stein, Senior Managing Director, please see the Astor Asset Management web site at www.astorllc.com.

About Knight

Knight Capital Group (NYSE Euronext: KCG) is a global financial services firm that provides access to the capital markets across multiple asset classes to a broad network of clients, including buy- and sell-side firms and corporations. Knight is headquartered in Jersey City, New Jersey, with a growing global presence across the Americas, Europe, and the Asia Pacific region.

ABOUT THE AUTHOR

Robert Stein is the Senior Managing Director and Head of Global Asset Management for Astor Asset Management and Knight Capital Group, Inc. He also serves as the Senior Portfolio Manager of Astor's separately managed account programs and the Astor Long/Short ETF. Rob started his career in 1983 as a project analyst for the Federal Reserve under the chairmanship of Paul Volcker. He then held senior trading or portfolio management positions with Bank of America New York, Harris Bank Chicago, and Continental Bank Chicago, which was acquired by Bank of America. In 1991, Rob became the Managing Director of Proprietary Trading at Barclay's Bank PLC, New York.

Returning to Chicago in 1994, he formed Astor Financial Inc. and later established Astor Asset Management, which provides investment advisory services to clients. Rob is also the author of The Bull Inside the Bear: Finding New Investment Opportunities in Today's Fast-Changing Economy and Inside Greenspan's Briefcase: Investment Strategies for Profiting from Reports and Data. He is regularly featured in print and broadcast media for the financial world, including the Wall Street Journal, Bloomberg BusinessWeek, Investor's Business Daily, ABC, FOX News, Bloomberg, and CNBC. Rob is the founder and president of the Dream of Jeanne Foundation and is the vice chairman of the board of trustees of Glenkirk, both of which help mentally challenged people participate in community life. Rob graduated from the University of Michigan and holds Series 3, 7, and 65 licenses.

GLOSSARY OF ECONOMIC TERMS

▲ ▲ ▲ ▲ ▲ ▲

There are a variety of indicators that reflect at least one aspect of the U.S. economy. Some of the indicators are broad measurements, such as Gross Domestic Product (GDP), which gauges the output of U.S. business. Others, such as Vehicle Sales, have a far more limited scope. Taken together, these indicators provide in-depth information about how the economy has been performing and a hint of what is likely to come.

At Astor Asset Management, our economics-based approach to active management requires that we closely monitor economic data. While we give more weight to some indicators (such as GDP and the Employment Situation) over others, each report offers some insight. The best way to make informed investment decisions is with a thorough understanding of the current state of the economy (expansion, peak, contraction, or trough) and the strength or weakness of that prevailing trend. We also believe that investment professionals and their savvy clientele should be familiar with economic reports and indicators, to understand their meaning and discern their relative importance.

Following is a glossary of economic reports, with a brief description of each.

Agricultural Prices

Released at the end of each month

This report from the U.S. Department of Agriculture includes the prices received by farmers for crops, livestock, and livestock products. Data are derived from surveys of mills and elevators (grain); packers, stockyards, auctions, dealers, and other sources (livestock); and sample surveys and market check data (fruits and vegetable prices).

Beige Book

Released eight times per year

Commonly known as the Beige Book, the Federal Reserve's "Summary of Commentary on Current Economic Conditions" is published eight times a year. Each Federal Reserve Bank gathers anecdotal information on current economic conditions in its district through reports from bank and branch directors and interviews with key business people, economists, market experts, and other sources. The Beige Book summarizes this information by district and sector. The Beige Book does not represent the views of the Federal Reserve Board or the Federal Reserve Banks, but summarizes comments from businesses and contacts outside of the Federal Reserve System.

Business Inventories

Released the middle of each month

This report from the Bureau of Census includes three components. Monthly Retail Trade presents data on dollar-value of retail sales and sales for selected establishment, as well as a sub-sample of firms providing data on end-of-month inventories. Monthly Wholesale Trade includes data on dollar values of merchant wholesalers' sales and end-of-month inventories. Manufacturers report current production levels and future production commitments, as well as the value of shipments, new orders net of cancellations, month-end total inventory, materials and supplies, work-in-process, and finished goods inventories.

Chain Store Sales

(see ICSC-Goldman Sachs Chain Store Sales Trends)

Challenger Report

Released during the first week of each month

The Challenger Report is a monthly job outlook report from outplacement firm Challenger, Gray & Christmas.

Chicago Fed National Activity Index

Released at the end of each month

The Chicago Fed National Activity Index, released monthly by the Chicago Federal Reserve Board, is a coincident indicator of broad economic activity. An index reading of "zero" indicates that the economy is growing at its long-run potential growth rate. A value above zero indicates that the economy is growing above potential, while a negative value indicates that the economy is growing below potential. The index is a weighted average of 85 indicators of national economic activity. These indicators are drawn from five broad categories of data: (1) production and income; (2) employment, unemployment, and hours worked; (3) personal consumption and housing; (4) manufacturing and trade sales; (5) inventories and orders.

Chicago Purchasing Managers Chicago Business Barometer

Released on the last business day of each month

This report provides a regional view of the national economy, summarizing current business activity. The report is also known as the Chicago Purchasing Manager Index or Chicago PMI.

Conference Board Consumer Confidence Index

Released at the end of each month

The Conference Board Consumer Confidence Index measures the level of confidence that individual households have in the performance of the economy. Survey questionnaires are mailed to a nationwide representative sample of households, which are asked five questions to rate the current business conditions in the household's area: business conditions six months into the future, job availability in the area, job availability in six months, and family income in six months. Responses are seasonally adjusted. An index is constructed for each response and then a composite index is fashioned based on the responses. Two other indices one to assess the present situation and one for expectations about the future—are also constructed. Expectations account for 60 percent of the index, while the current situation is responsible for the remaining 40 percent.

Conference Board Employment Trends Index

Released on the Monday following the Friday release of the Employment Situation Report

The Employment Trends Index combines eight labor-market indicators. This index includes: percentage of respondents who report jobs are hard to get; initial claims for unemployment insurance; percentage of firms with positions they are unable to fill now; number of employees hired by temporary help industry; workers with part-time jobs due to economic reasons; job openings; industrial production; and manufacturing and trade sales.

Conference Board Help Wanted OnLine Data Series

Released at the end of each month

The Conference Board **HELP WANTED ONLINE** Data Series measures the number of new, first-time online jobs and jobs reposted from the previous month on more than 1,200 major Internet job sites and smaller job sites that serve niche markets and smaller geographic areas. The new online series is not a direct measure of job vacancies. The level of ads in print and online can change for reasons not related to overall job demand.

Conference Board Leading Economic Index

Released mid-month each month

This index is designed to signal peaks and troughs in the business cycle. The leading, coincident, and lagging economic indexes are essentially composite averages of several individual leading, coincident, or lagging indicators. They are constructed to summarize and reveal common turning point patterns in economic data in a clearer and more convincing manner than any individual component—primarily because they smooth out some of the volatility of individual components.

Conference Board Measure of CEO Confidence

Released quarterly, during the first week after each quarter closes

The Conference Board Measure of CEO Confidence assesses CEO views of economic conditions. The report includes assessments of current conditions as well as the outlook for improvement and/or decline.

Construction Spending

Released on the first day of each month

Construction Spending, from the Bureau of Census, reports the dollar value of newly completed structures. Individual data series are available for several residential building types; nonresidential private building types; public buildings, and other public and private structures, such as roads and utility lines. Both current dollar and inflation-adjusted estimates are available. This release is used directly to estimate the investment in the structures component of the expenditures estimate of GDP. Since a building is not recorded in the data series until it is completed, this series is a lagging indicator of construction activity.

Consumer Confidence Survey

(See Conference Board's Consumer Confidence Survey)

Consumer Credit

Released on the fifth business day of each month

Consumer Credit, from the Federal Reserve Board, represents loans for households for financing consumer purchases of goods and services and for refinancing existing consumer debt. Secured and unsecured loans are included except those secured with real estate (mortgages, home equity loans and lines, etc). Securitized consumer loans, loans made by finance companies, banks, and retailers that are sold as securities are included. The two categories of consumer credit are revolving and non-revolving debt. Revolving debt covers credit card use whether for purchases or for cash advances, store charge accounts, and check credit plans that allow overdrafts up to certain amounts on personal accounts.

Consumer Price Index (CPI)

Released on the fifteenth of each month

The Consumer Price Index (CPI) is a measure of the average change over time in the prices paid by urban consumers for a fixed market basket of consumer goods and services. The CPI report, released by the Bureau of Labor Statistics, provides a way for consumers to compare what the market basket of goods and services costs this month with what the same market basket cost a month or a year ago. The CPI reports price changes in over 200 categories, arranged into eight major groups. The CPI includes various user fees such as water and sewerage charges, auto registration fees, vehicle tolls, and so forth. Taxes that are directly associated with the prices of specific goods and services (such as sales and excise taxes) are also included.

Consumer Sentiment Survey

(See Thomson Reuters/University of Michigan Survey of Consumers)

Current Account Deficit Report

Released quarterly, mid-month

The Current Account report from the Bureau of Economic Analysis reflects the movement of non-capital items in the balance of payments account. The report breaks out the balance on goods, services, and income. Changes in the current account balance are a useful barometer for the state of U.S. foreign trade as well as the flow of investment to and from the United States. A widening deficit on the current account is typical when the United States is purchasing excessive imports. The current account also provides a good measure of the performance of the United States in the international markets.

Durable Goods

Released at the end of each month

Durable Goods from the Bureau of the Census is the advance release of overall factory orders and shipments. Durable goods are industrial products with an expected life of one year or more. They include intermediate goods, such as steel, lumber, and electronic components; finished industrial machinery and equipment; and finished consumer durable goods, such as furniture, autos, and TVs. Data are reported for seven different industry groupings, plus the total. New orders are the dollar volume of orders for new products received by domestic manufacturers from any source, domestic or foreign.

ECRI Weekly Leading Index

Released each Friday

The Economic Cycle Research Institute's (ECRI) Weekly Leading Index is a weighted average of seven key economic data designed to predict economic conditions in the near term. Meant to be clearly cyclical, the index is designed to turn down before a recession and turn up before an expansion.

Employment Cost Index

Released quarterly on the last Thursday of the reporting month

The Employment Cost Index (ECI) from the Bureau of Labor Statistics is based on a survey of employer payrolls. The index measures the change in the cost of labor, free from the influence of employment shifts among occupations and industries.

Employment Situation

Released on the first Friday of each month

Payroll figures are reported each month by the Bureau of Labor Statistics in its Employment Situation Report. Payroll employment is a measure of the number of jobs in more than 500 industries, except for farming, in all states and 255 metropolitan areas. The employment estimates are based on a survey of larger businesses. The report also provides information on average weekly hours worked and average hourly earnings, which are important indicators of the tightness of labor markets. An index of aggregate weekly hours worked is also included in the release, which gives an important early indication of production before the quarterly GDP numbers come out.

Existing Home Sales

Released around the twenty-fifth of each month

Each month the National Association of Realtors (NAR) Research Division receives data on existing single-family home sales from over 650 boards and associations of realtors and multiple listing systems across the country. This data is included in the Existing Home Sales Report.

Factory Orders

Released during the first week of each month

The Factory Orders report from the Bureau of the Census includes the dollar volume of new orders, shipments, unfilled orders, and inventories reported by domestic manufacturers. Data are reported for numerous industry groupings, plus the total and specialized aggregates. New orders are a good measure of demand for each industry and in aggregate, and shipments are a good measure of supply. Unfilled orders are the backlog of orders that have been received by domestic manufacturers, but not yet shipped. Unfilled orders are one indication of the balance between demand and supply, most often used to indicate an excess of demand relative to supply.

Federal Open Market Committee (FOMC) Meeting

Meets eight times per year

The Federal Open Market Committee of the Federal Reserve Board (FOMC) meets approximately every six weeks to consider whether any changes need to be made to monetary policy. The FOMC is comprised of the seven Federal Reserve Board members, including the current chairman, and five Federal Reserve District Bank presidents.

FOMC Minutes

Minutes of regularly scheduled meetings are released three weeks after the date of the FOMC meeting

The Federal Open Market Committee (FOMC) holds eight regularly scheduled meetings during the year and other meetings as needed.

Gross Domestic Product (GDP)

Released on the last Friday of each month

Gross Domestic Product (GDP) is a measure of the total production and consumption of goods and services in the United States. The report, released by the Bureau of Economic Analysis, includes two complementary measures of GDP, one based on income and one based on expenditures. GDP is measured one way by adding up the labor, capital, and tax costs of producing the output. On the consumption side, GDP is measured by adding up expenditures by households, businesses, government, and net foreign purchases. Theoretically, these two measures should be equal. However, due to problems collecting the data, there is often a discrepancy between the two measures. The GDP price deflator is used to convert output measured at current prices into constant-dollar GDP.

ICSC-Goldman Sachs (ICSC-GS) Chain-Store Sales Index
Released each Tuesday

The index measures nominal same-store or comparable-store sales excluding restaurant and vehicle demand. The weekly index statistically represents industry sales. The standard period used for the index is Sunday through Saturday. The weekly sales index is presented on an adjusted basis to account for normal seasonality and to counter other data anomalies.

Import and Export Prices
Released mid-month each month

Every month, the Bureau of Labor Statistics collects net transaction prices for more than 20,000 products from over 6,000 companies and secondary sources to formulate the Import and Export Prices report. The overall import price index measures the price change of products purchased from other countries by U.S. residents. The overall export price index measures the change in the prices of domestically produced U.S. goods shipped to other countries.

Industrial Production/Capacity Utilization
Released around the fifteenth of each month

The Industrial Production index, released by the Federal Reserve Board, measures the change in output in U.S. manufacturing, mining, and electric and gas utilities. Output refers to the physical quantity of items produced. The index covers the production of goods and power for domestic sales in the United States and for export. It excludes production in the agriculture, construction, transportation, communication, trade, finance, and service industries; government output, and imports. Each component is weighted according to its relative importance in the base period. The report also includes Capacity Utilization, which gauges how much available capacity exists. The greater the capacity utilization, the higher the production level, which could indicate inflation (typically a measurement over 85 percent). Conversely, a low capacity number indicates economic weakness as industries are producing below their potential.

International Trade

Released around the ninth to the thirteenth of each month

The International Trade report from the Department of Commerce reflects the balance of trade, or the difference between exports and imports of goods and services. Merchandise data are provided for U.S. total foreign trade with all nations, with detail for trade with particular nations and regions of the world, as well as for individual commodities. Using the report, the importance of one country's economy may be analyzed in terms of U.S. trade. The report can further reveal to what extent overseas growth is contributing to the U.S. economic performance.

ISM Report

(See Manufacturing ISM Report on Business)

ISM Non-Manufacturing Index

(See Non-Manufacturing ISM Report on Business)

Jobless Claims

(See Unemployment Insurance Weekly Claims Report)

Job Opening and Labor Turnover

Released around the tenth of each month

The Job Openings and Labor Turnover Survey (JOLTS) is released by the Bureau of Labor Statistics (BLS). Data in the survey are collected and compiled monthly from a sample of business establishments. Data are collected for total employment, job openings, hiring, employees quitting, layoffs and discharges, and other separations.

Kansas City Fed Manufacturing Survey

Released on the last Thursday of each month

The Federal Reserve Bank of Kansas City surveys roughly 300 manufacturing plants that are representative of the district's industrial and geographic makeup. Indices are calculated by subtracting the percentage of total respondents reporting decreases in a given indicator from the percentage of those reporting increases. The indices, which can range from 100 to -100, reveal the general direction of the indicators by showing how, or if, the number of plants with improving conditions offset those with worsening conditions. Index values greater than zero generally suggest expansion, while values less than zero indicate contraction.

Manufacturing ISM Report on Business

Released on the first business day of each month

This report is based on data compiled from purchasing and supply executives nationwide across multiple industries. According to ISM, a reading above 50 percent indicates expansion in manufacturing, while a reading below 50 percent indicates a general decline.

Manufacturing and Trade Inventories and Sales Report

Released around the fifteenth of each month

This U.S. Census Bureau report includes distributive trade sales and manufacturers' shipments (sales); manufacturers' and trade inventories (inventories); and total business inventories/sales ratio. Estimates are based on data from three surveys: the Monthly Retail Trade Survey, the Monthly Wholesale Trade Survey, and the Manufacturers' Shipments, Inventories, and Orders Survey.

Monster.com Employment Index

Released during the first week of each month

The Monster.com Employment Index is a comprehensive monthly analysis of online job demand from Monster Worldwide, Inc. This index provides a snapshot of online recruitment nationwide.

Monthly Mass Layoffs

Released around the twentieth to the twenty-third of each month

Mass layoff statistics are compiled by the Bureau of Labor Statistics from initial unemployment insurance claims. Each month, states report on establishments that have at least 50 initial unemployment insurance claims filed against them during a consecutive five-week period, regardless of duration. These establishments then are contacted by the state agency to determine whether these separations lasted 31 days or longer, and, if so, other information concerning the layoff is collected. Quarterly mass layoff reports include additional information. The report lists how many layoff events occurred and how many people who are eligible to receive unemployment compensation were affected. Layoff events are segmented by state and industry.

Monthly Retail Trade and Food Services

Released around the twelfth of each month

This report from the U.S. Census Bureau provides an early estimate of monthly sales for retail and food service in the U.S. The survey is based on questionnaires sent to approximately 5,000 firms.

Monthly Treasury Statement

Released mid-month each month

The U.S. Department of Treasury budget is a monthly account of the surplus or deficit of the U.S. government. Detailed information is provided on receipts and outlays of the federal government. The information is provided on a monthly and fiscal year-to-date basis.

Mortgage Bankers Association's Weekly Mortgage Applications Survey

Released each Wednesday

The Mortgage Bankers Association's (MBA) Weekly Applications Survey analyzes mortgage application activity. The survey is used as an indicator of housing and mortgage finance activity.

NAHB/Wells Fargo Housing Market Index

Released mid-month each month

This index is based on a monthly survey of National Association of Home Builders (NAHB) members on the single-family housing market. The survey asks respondents to rate current market conditions for the sale of new homes and conditions in the next six months, as well as the traffic of prospective buyers.

New Home Sales

Released around the twenty-third to the twenty-fifth of each month

The Bureau of the Census compiles data for this report from sample surveys. The report includes sales figures and median prices of housing.

New Residential Construction

Released on the third Thursday of each month

New Residential Construction, released by the Bureau of the Census, provides statistics on the construction of new privately owned residential structures in the United States. Data include the number of new housing units authorized by building permits; the number of housing units authorized to be built, but not yet started; the number of housing units started; the number of housing units under construction; and the number of housing units completed.

Non-Manufacturing ISM Report on Business

Released on the third business day of each month

This index is based on data compiled from purchasing and supply executives nationwide. The index based on four indicators: business activity, new orders, employment, and supplier deliveries. According to ISM, an index reading above 50 percent indicates that the non-manufacturing economy in that index is generally expanding; below 50 percent indicates that it is generally declining. For supplier deliveries, a reading above 50 percent indicates slower deliveries and below 50 percent indicates faster deliveries.

NY Fed Empire State Manufacturing Survey

Released mid-month each month

This report is based on a monthly survey of manufacturers in New York State conducted by the Federal Reserve Bank of New York.

Personal Income

Released around the first or last business day of each month

The Personal Income report from the Bureau of Economic Analysis mainly measures the income received by households from employment, self-employment, investments, and transfer payments. It also includes small amounts for expenses of nonprofit organizations and income of certain fiduciary activities. The largest component of personal income is wages and salaries from employment. Personal income is released after the employment report and thus can be estimated by the payroll and earnings data for the employment report. Disposable income refers to personal income after the payment of income, estate, certain other taxes, and payments to governments.

Philadelphia Fed Business Outlook Survey

Released mid-month each month

Every month, the Federal Reserve Bank of Philadelphia surveys respondents to assess general business conditions as well as company business conditions. Answers are given based in the current month versus the previous month, and the outlook for six months from the current month. An indicator is presented for a decrease, no change, an increase, and a diffusion index.

Producer Price Index (PPI)

Released during the third week of each month

The Producer Price Index (PPI) from the Bureau of Labor Statistics is a family of indices that measures average changes in selling prices received by domestic producers for their output. The PPI tracks changes in prices for nearly every goods-producing industry in the domestic economy, including agriculture, electricity and natural gas, forestry, fisheries, manufacturing, and mining.

Productivity and Costs

Released quarterly, at the beginning of the month

Productivity and associated costs, compiled by the Bureau of Labor Statistics, reflects the relationship between real output and the labor and capital inputs involved in production. This shows changes over time in the amount of goods and services produced per unit of input.

Retail Sales

(See Monthly Retail Trade and Food Services)

Richmond Fed Survey of Manufacturing Activity

Released at the end of each month

The Federal Reserve Bank of Richmond surveys manufacturing plants that are representative of the district's industrial and geographic make-up. The indices are calculated by subtracting the percentage of total respondents reporting decreases in a given indicator from the percentage of those reporting increases. The indices, which can range from 100 to -100, reveal the general direction of the indicators by showing how the number of plants with improving conditions offset those with worsening conditions. Index values greater than zero generally suggest expansion, while values less than zero indicate contraction.

Semiconductor Book-to-Bill Ratio

Released around the fifteenth to the twentieth of each month

Semiconductor Equipment and Materials International releases the results of a survey of U.S. manufacturers on a monthly basis. The 3-month moving average of shipments and new orders plus their ratio, named the book-to-bill ratio, are all included.

Semiconductor Billing

First of last day of the month

The Semiconductor Industry Association reports the global dollar volume of integrated circuit sales on a three-month moving average on a monthly basis. All types of semiconductor chips are included in the totals: microprocessors, memory, and others. The sales are reported individually for four regions: North America, Asia-Pacific, Japan, and Europe. The data are compiled from a survey of the largest global chip manufacturers.

Thomson Reuters/University of Michigan Survey of Consumers

Released on the first or last day of each month

The Thomson Reuters/University of Michigan Consumer Sentiment Survey is based upon a nationally representative sample of consumer households. It reports an index of consumer sentiment and an index of consumer expectations.

Treasury Budget

(see Monthly Treasury Statement)

Unemployment Insurance Weekly Claims Report

Released each Thursday

This weekly report from the Department of Labor measures the number of applicants filing for state jobless benefits. The report is important as an indicator of employment and, therefore, economic trends. An increase in jobless claims, for example, shows that job prospects are worsening (or at least have not improved), while a decrease in claims indicates job growth. On a week-to-week basis, the claims number can be volatile. Therefore, looking at jobless claims over a longer time period (such as month-to-month) may be more meaningful.

Unemployment Rate

Released on the first Friday of each month

The unemployment rate is released by the Bureau of Labor Statistics, and represents the number unemployed as a percent of the labor force. Persons are classified as unemployed if they do not have a job, have actively looked for work in the prior four weeks, and are currently available for work. Actively looking for work may consist of any of the following activities: networking, contacting an employer directly, or having a job interview with public or private employment agency; contacting a school or university employment center; sending out resumes or filling out applications; placing or answering advertisements; checking union or professional registers; or some other means of active job search. People are counted as employed if they did any work at all for pay or profit during the survey week. This includes all part-time and temporary work, as well as regular full-time year-round employment. Persons also are counted as employed if they have a job at which they did not work during the survey week because they were on vacation, experiencing child-care problems, taking care of some other family or personal obligation, on maternity or paternity leave; involved in an industrial dispute; or prevented from working by bad weather.

Vehicle Sales

Released during the first week of each month

Auto companies report vehicle sales each month. Light vehicle sales are divided between cars and light trucks (sport utility vehicles, pickup trucks, and vans). Light vehicle sales include both sales of vehicles assembled in North America that are sold in the United States and sales of imported vehicles sold in the United States.

Weekly Natural Gas Storage Report

Released each Thursday

This report from the U.S. Energy Information Administration provides data on working gas in underground storage in the lower 48 states, including current storage and historic comparisons.

Wells Fargo/Gallup Investor and Retirement Optimism Index

Released quarterly

The index draws from investors randomly selected from across the country. An investor is defined as a person who is head of a household or a spouse in a household with total savings and investments of $10,000 or more. The sample size is comprised of roughly two-thirds non-retired people and one-third retirees.

Wholesale Trade

Released around the tenth of each month

Companies provide data to the Bureau of Census on dollar-values of merchant wholesale sales, end-of-month inventories, and methods of inventory valuation. Monthly wholesale trade, sales, and inventories reports are released six weeks after the close of the reference month. They contain preliminary current month figures and final figures for the previous month. Statistics include sales, inventories, and stock or sale ratios. Data are collected from selected wholesale firms. The sample is updated every quarter to add new businesses and eliminate those who are no longer active wholesalers.

ECONOMIC CALENDAR

Monday	Tuesday	Wednesday	Thursday	Friday
	1 Semiconductor Billings 1 Challenger Report 2 Construction Spending 2 Manufacturing ISM Index 3 ICSC - Goldman Sachs chain store sales 2 Personal Income 3	**2** Vehicle Sales - AutoData 1 MBA Mortgage Applications Survey 1 Conference Board Measure of CEO confidence 2	**3** Chain Store Sales 3 Monster Employment Index 2 Jobless Claims 4 Productivity and Costs 3 Factory Orders 2 Non-Mfg. ISM Index 4 Oil and Gas Inventories 2 Weekly Natural Gas Storage Report 2	**4** Employment Situation 5 ECRI Weekly Leading Index 1
7 Consumer Credit 1 Conference Board Employment Trends Index 2	**8** Chain Store Sales ICSC Goldman Sachs 2	**9** MBA Mortgage Applications Survey 2 Job Openings and Labor Turnover Survey 2 Wholesale Trade (MWTR) 3 Oil and Gas Inventories 2	**10** Jobless Claims 4 Import and Export Prices 2 Weekly Natural Gas Storage Report 2 Treasury Budget 3	**11** ECRI Weekly Leading Index 1

Scale: 1 – Least Significant; 3 – Signficant; 5 – Highly Signficant

Monday	Tuesday	Wednesday	Thursday	Friday
14	**15**	**16**	**17**	**18**
Retail Sales (MARTS) 3	ICSC GOldman Sachs Chain Store Sales Snapshot 2	MBA Mortgage Applications Survey 2	Jobless Claims 4	Current Account 3
International Trade 2	Consumer Price Index 3	Industrial Production 2	The Conference Board Leading Indicators 1	ECRI Weekly Leading Index 1
	Business Inventories (MTIS) 2	Oil and Gas Inventories 2	Weekly Natural Gas Storage Report 2	Producer Price Index 3
	NY Empire State Manufacturing Survey 2	Beige Book 4	Philadelphia Fed Survey 2	
	NAHB Wells Fargo Housing Market Index 2		SEMI Book-to-Bill Ratio 2	
	Manufacturing and Trade Inventories and sales 2		New Residential Construction 1	
21	**22**	**23**	**24**	**25**
	ICSC Goldman Sachs Chain Store Sales 2	MBA Mortgage Applications Survey 2	Jobless Claims 4	GDP 5
		Monthly Mass Layoffs 3	Durable Goods 3	Existing Home Sales 2
		Oil and Gas Inventories 2	The Conference Board Help Wanted 2	ECRI Weekly Leading Index 1
			New Home Sales 2	
			Weekly Natural Gas Storage Report 2	
			Kansas City Fed Manufacturing Survey 2	

Scale: 1 – Least Significant; 3 – Signficant; 5 – Highly Signficant